Make Your Menus Delicious, Nutritious Feasts with . . . The *Woman's Day* ® *Book of New Mexican Cooking!*

Imagine yourself serving mouth-watering, award-winning New Mexican cuisine! Thanks to Jane Butel, the woman behind Pecos Valley Spice Valley Company and one of America's most trusted authorities on New Mexican, Southwestern and Tex-Mex cooking, your opportunity is here.

Now you can prepare and serve creative, economical, flavor-perfect dishes—from tasty appetizers to spicy beginner's beef tacos, to pollo en mole verde (chicken in green chile sauce), to refreshing desserts—and please even the most demanding palates.

There are complete buffet menus offered for all four seasons to make any party a sure hit. And the fresh ingredients you can't do without are easily available through a comprehensive mail-order listing.

The *Woman's Day* ® *Book of New Mexican Cooking*

will become your most treasured cookbook!

Woman's Day®
BOOK OF
NEW MEXICAN COOKING

JANE BUTEL

PUBLISHED BY POCKET BOOKS NEW YORK

Another *Original* publication of POCKET BOOKS

 POCKET BOOKS, a division of Simon & Schuster, Inc.
1230 Avenue of the Americas, New York, N.Y. 10020

ISBN: 0-671-44672-X

First Pocket Books printing March, 1984

10 9 8 7 6 5 4 3 2 1

POCKET and colophon are registered trademarks
of Simon & Schuster, Inc.

Printed in the U.S.A.

TO
AMY and CAROLE
For your always
ready . . . love, help,
kindness . . . and understanding.

Contents

TORTILLAS/SPECIALTIES

CHILE DISHES

SOUTHWESTERN HOSPITALITY

Introduction

Tex-Mex, or New Mexican, foods are fun, happy, colorful foods that reflect their sunny, earthy beginnings. When Columbus took his first mouthful of this piquant cuisine, he became very excited because he thought he had found the ultimate source for pepper and exotic spices.

The great popularity these fiesta foods are now experiencing has inspired new flavor combinations, innovative adaptations of traditional recipes, and creative serving ideas. When most people hear the term "Tex-Mex," they think of tacos, enchiladas, burritos, and the like. The Southwestern, New Mexican cuisine this book is all about stands apart from Mexican cooking in its clearer, more subtly spicy flavors. Tex-Mex food is of *New* Mexican origin, where the strong Spanish influence of the conquistadores on the ancient culture of the Pueblo Indians formed the basis for a new cuisine. And, of course, we "gringos" have added our own touches.

I am personally dedicated to savoring and developing new taste sensations to please the fiery passions of my palate and the palates of all other chile cultists who share this pleasure. I also devote much time and effort to experimenting with new mild and soothing accompaniments to complement the hot, spicy food.

I have eaten in many fine Tex-Mex, New Mex, and just plain Mexican restaurants, but I still find that—with rare exceptions—the home-cooked specialties are best. Why? Because so much more care is taken in the blending of fresh ingredients to produce the clear, fresh, and pungent flavors that make Southwestern food so intriguing.

It is the cook, armed with patience, a creative palate, and boundless curiosity, who is the primary ingredient in all wonderful food. And it is to these cooks that I dedicate this book.

Woman's Day®
BOOK OF
NEW
MEXICAN
COOKING

Ingredients

Chile

The temper, taste, and unique personality of Southwest American food relies heavily on the use of domestic chiles. Most varieties of chiles used for sauces and rellenos stuffing were hybridized within the last few decades in the agricultural experiment stations of New Mexico and California universities. They are popularly used both in the green, unripe form as well as in the red, sun-ripened form.

Green chiles are the basis for rellenos, relishes, and stews. Before eating these chiles, they must be parched and peeled. The greatest flavor comes from fresh or frozen chiles, as opposed to canned. Canning does not enhance good chile flavor; an overwhelmingly metallic, tinny taste results which detracts from the tart spiciness of any chile. When selecting green chiles, remember that the broader the shoulders, the blunter the tip, and the lighter the color, the milder the flavor.

Red chiles are sun-ripened green chiles. They are generally ground or crushed and used as the flavor base for sauces, stews, and main dishes. Every fall in New Mexico, chiles are traditionally threaded onto strings or loops known as ristras and hung to sun dry. These brilliant, red ristras adorning the adobe houses are absolutely breathtaking against the piercing blue skies. Native cooks leave the chiles intact on the ristras, using them to decorate their kitchens. They pull off the desired amount of dried chiles, crush them, bake slightly, stew, and then strain them. Alternatively, some native cooks prefer to stew the whole, dried chiles until the tough outer shell loosens (about 30 minutes); then they strain them and use them for Caribe (page 53).

More convenient to use are the pure ground or crushed red chiles. The challenge has always been to find them. Look for packages of pure powdered chile. Some companies add 40% salt and 20% chemicals, additives, and flavorings to the chiles, greatly limiting the powder's use in creating sauces or varying flavor blends.

When cooking with chiles, always use a mild California or Anaheim variety to create the flavor base. The hotter New Mexico types, either ground or caribe, are added to build heat.

Other popular varieties of chiles used in Tex-Mex/New Mex cooking are:

Pequín

The original mother of all chiles. Thumbnail-sized and rarely cultivated, pequín is harvested along the Mexican border from native plants and is sought for its hot, fiery taste. The term *quebrado,* meaning crushed, is traditionally used to describe pequín.

Jalapeño

Very popular for its intense heat with a full, tart chile flavor. These chiles are oval-shaped, dark green, and thick-fleshed. Rarely sold fresh except in the Southwest, they are very popular when sold pickled. Look for the home-canned or jarred varieties pickled in a vinegar solution, rather than those preserved in heavy oil, which is less flavorful. Fresh jalapeños are best when parched and peeled (see page 13) since the skins are very tough.

Serrano Chiles

Lighter green than jalapeños, these chiles are small, narrow, and intensely hot. They possess little flavor, just incredible heat. Increasingly sold fresh, serrano chiles are also available canned.

Southwest Spices

Most of the herbs and spices used in New Mexican cooking are native to the sunny slopes. The most popular traditional seasonings are native Mexican oregano, onions, salt, and garlic.

More recently popular, and particularly complementary to chiles, is cumin (or comino). Not grown in the Southwest, it was probably introduced by the Spanish.

Less well-known, but still popular seasonings are anise, bay leaf, fresh cilantro leaves, and coriander, the dried seeds of cilantro. (In Spanish, all coriander, leaves as well as seeds, is known as cilantro.) Sage and yerba bueno (wild mint) are the other most popular seasonings.

Cheese

The most widely used cheeses are Monterey Jack and Cheddar. Monterey Jack was developed in Monterey, California about fifty years ago by blending the soft, easy-melting mozzarella with a full cream Cheddar; it has become my overall favorite because of its easy-melting quality and its mild, yet sharp-edged, flavor. The California Jack is softer (usually with a paraffin rind) than the firmer, somewhat sharper-flavored Wisconsin Jack and can be difficult to grate unless partially frozen.

Cheddar, sharp to mild, full cream or partially milk-based, is all good with chile cookery. I often prefer a 50/50 blend of coarsely grated Monterey Jack and Cheddar for toppings on such dishes as tacos, chile con carne, and enchiladas.

Garlic

Fresh minced or crushed garlic is extremely popular in Southwestern cooking. For the best flavor, *do not* substitute garlic powder or salt.

Onions

Sharp-flavored Spanish onions are best for all cooking uses. The sweeter Bermuda types should be reserved for salads.

Avocados

The knobby, black-skinned Haas avocado or the black and bright green Fuertes avocado is best for guacamole and garnishing. The large, bright green, smooth-skinned varieties are too sweet and watery for best flavor in southwestern cooking. Always plan at least 3 to 5 days ahead when preparing avocado dishes; very often the fruits need a few days' ripening time after they are purchased. Ripen hard avocados in a warm place out of direct sunlight. Watch carefully. When you press gently with your thumb and an indentation remains, they are ripe and should be refrigerated until ready to use. The flesh should be buttery and easy to slice.

The easiest way to peel an avocado is to score the outer skin, top to bottom, and then pull each section down with a knife or the back of a spoon. If you plan to mash or chop the avocado, simply slice it in half, remove the pit, and scoop out the flesh with a spoon. Always prepare avocados at the last moment, as they darken quickly. The best way to control discoloration is to use a sprinkle of fresh lime juice (use lemon juice only if lime is unavailable); then cover tightly with cellophane wrap, eliminating all air. If trying to keep guacamole, place in the smallest possible dish or container and seal the top.

Beans

The brown-speckled, whitish grey pinto beans are most often used for stewing and refrying. Their nutlike, full flavor is best when they are freshly cooked or frozen. Kidney beans are sometimes used, especially in California and Arizona.

Shortening

Lard or bacon drippings are the traditional favorites for use as an ingredient as well as for frying; the most authentic texture and flavor are obtained when they are used. If health or other preferences prevent their use, substitute solid shortening, margarine, or butter when baking. Use butter or margarine as a substitute when sautéing, when creating a roux base for sauces, and in chile con carne. Cooking oil is the best substitute when deep frying.

Masa

Lime-treated corn, whether white, yellow, or blue, was ground with lava wheels in the old days to create masa. Today, most commercial masa is machine-milled. The best flavor results from careful processing—repeated rinsing to remove most of the residual lime and fine milling to create a smooth, flourlike texture. Dry masa is generally available in most food markets in the Southwest and is sold prepared at tortilla factories. In other areas of the country, it is stocked in Mexican or Latin American grocery stores and in gourmet specialty stores.

Equipment

Authentic southwestern cookery requires very little special equipment. You can become a master of the cuisine with a modest investment. Traditional tools, such as the tortilla press, a taco fryer, tostado fryer, and bolillo are relatively inexpensive and fun to use. Appliances, such as food processors, blenders, and mixers, create added convenience; and microwave or convection ovens are terrific for speeding up such cooking processes as baking and melting cheese. You might consider investing in an electric deep-fat fryer. The thermostatic control assures even browning of temperature-delicate foods such as sopaipillas and taco shells, which makes the expense totally worthwhile. Lacking this appliance, an accurate frying thermometer is critical. If these various Tex-Mex appliances and equipment are unavailable to you locally, check Mail Order Sources (page 237).

Tortilla Press

This is a real boon to making smooth, even corn tortillas. Recently, American gourmet equipment manufacturers have begun designing and marketing more convenient and efficient models. Look for smooth interior surfaces, a diameter of 6 to 7 inches and a strong, well-designed lever to pull down for flattening the tortillas.

Bolillo

A short rolling pin that is a uniform 2 inches in diameter and 8 or more inches long. It fits ideally in the palm and rolls wheat tortillas to a uniform thinness. I find the rustic type with no handles the easiest to work with. The bolillo is also perfect for rolling empanada and bizcochito dough.

Tapa

Used for baking tortillas over high heat for rapid browning. In New Mexico, the traditional tapas are former cast-iron stove inserts. A cast-iron griddle, skillet, or other dark, heat-absorbing surface is best. Do not allow a fast-talking salesperson to sell you a shiny model . . . they are useless! *Comal* is the Mexican/Spanish name for a tapa.

Taco Fryer

Look for a model that will hold the tortillas in a "U" shape while immersed in deep, hot fat. For home use, the most practical type will have a double taco holder at the end of a tonglike handle. Some multiple taco fryer models simply do not work— the holders for the tortillas float away, allowing the tortillas to release from the bottom of the frying mechanism.

Molinillo

A long-handled, wooden utensil with rather intricate interlocking circles on the end. When rubbed between the palms, the circles create a very effective whipping action that is ideal for blending and foaming hot Mexican chocolate or soft custards as they cook.

Appetizers

A variety of colorful, often crisp, highly textured or spiced snacks and appetizers abound in the border states; many are original Tex-Mex creations while others were developed south of the border. Taste sensations range from fiery hot to cool and refreshing.

Appetizers can be elaborate or very simple. One of the simplest and yet deliciously pleasing is a basket of freshly fried tostadas served with assorted salsas for dipping. The secret here is deep frying your own corn tortillas; they are simple to make and are infinitely better than the commercially prepared varieties (unless, of course, you can find the homemade-type tostadas).

Guacamole, nachos, chile con queso, carnitas, chile nuts, frijole dip, beef jerky, and ceviche are some of my favorite starters. You'll be amazed at the pleasures derived from the possible combinations of chiles, onions, meats, vegetables, tomatoes, garlic, and cheese.

TOSTADAS (CORN TORTILLA CHIPS)

Commercial chips are never this good! Tostadas will freeze very well in a tightly sealed rigid container for up to 6 months.

Yield: 48 tostadas

Lard or oil for deep frying
12 freshly made corn tortillas
Salt, optional

1. In a heavy pan, heat lard or oil 2 inches deep to 375°F.
2. Using a sharp knife or kitchen shears, cut tortillas in quarters, pinwheel fashion, leaving the center portion uncut. This will make turning them in the hot fat easier.
3. Deep fry tortillas, one at a time, until crisp; turn once. Drain on paper towelling and break into quarters. Sprinkle lightly with salt, if desired. Serve warm or at room temperature.

VARIATION: For mexi-chips, sprinkle with crushed fresh garlic, ground pure hot chile, and cumin.

TRADITIONAL NACHOS

A true southwestern creation, nachos are spicy and versatile.

Yield: 36

36 tostadas
36 small squares of Cheddar or Monterey Jack cheese
4 jalapeño chiles, sliced thinly into rings

1. Place tostadas on a baking sheet; top each one with a piece of cheese and with one or more slices of jalapeño chile.
2. Broil for 5 minutes or until the cheese melts.

VARIATIONS: Some finely chopped scallions are a nice addition. Or place a spoonful of frijoles refritos or bean dip under the cheese. You may substitute fresh salsa or salsa verde for jalapeño chiles. To make "pull apart" nachos, spread tostados in a single layer so that they touch each other on an oven-proof platter. Sprinkle evenly with grated cheese and jalapeño chiles, adding a few spoonsful of refried beans, if desired, and bake at 425°F for about 5 minutes, or until cheese melts.

NACHOS GRANDE

Unlimited variations can make this platter sensationally different every time it's prepared. Let your imagination and what's on hand in your refrigerator be your guide!

½ pound chorizo sausage
½ pound tostadas
Large oven-proof platter
3 cups refried beans
Sliced jalapeño chiles to taste
1½ to 2 cups grated combined Monterey Jack and Cheddar
  cheese
1 recipe Guacamole (page 26)
1 cup sour cream, approximately
¼ cup thinly sliced scallions or Spanish onion
½ cup sliced pitted black olives
Red or green salsa (pages 52, 55)

1. Brown and thoroughly cook crumbled chorizo; slice and set aside. Preheat oven to 425°F.
2. Spread a generous layer of tostada chips on an oven-proof platter. Spoon dollops of refried beans on top of tostadas; then sprinkle jalapeño slices to suit your taste. Sprinkle grated cheese over all.
3. Place in oven and bake about 10 to 15 minutes, until cheese is melted and beans are hot. Remove from oven, arrange chorizo around edges, spoon dollops of guacamole and sour cream on top, sprinkle with scallions and olive slices, and spoon some salsa over all.
4. Serve hot with extra salsa on the side.

VARIATION: In place of chorizo, you can use Chile con Carne (page 131) or beef, pork, or chicken taco fillings.

SOUTHWEST "PIZZAS"

Similar to nachos grande, these are larger, yet quick and easy to make. They are delicious as appetizers and can be served for a light lunch or late supper. Children love to make them! These "pizzas" are sometimes called cheese crisps.

1. Begin with crisp-fried whole, corn tortillas, warmed in a 300°F oven for 5 minutes.
2. Top with a combination of some of the following:

> fried, crumbled chorizo sausage, Italian sausage, or bulk pork sausage
> very thinly sliced onions or scallions
> refried beans
> green chiles, cut in strips
> chile con queso
> grated Monterey Jack or Cheddar cheese
> chile beef
> salsa verde, red salsa, or salsa fresca
> meat fillings such as chicken or pork

3. Bake in a preheated 450°F oven for about 5 minutes until heated through.

GUACAMOLE

Because texture is very important in this particular recipe, the avocados are not mashed, but are coarsely chopped. Guacamole is traditionally served with tostadas for dunking.

Yield: about 2 cups

2 ripe avocados
½ teaspoon salt
1 clove garlic, finely minced
1 teaspoon freshly squeezed lime juice, or to taste
1 medium-size tomato, chopped
¼ cup finely chopped Spanish onion
1 tablespoon finely chopped pickled jalapeño chile, or 2
    tablespoons chopped green chiles

1. Halve the avocados; scoop pulp into a bowl. *Coarsely* chop with a pastry blender or with two knives.
2. Add salt and garlic; then slowly add lime juice to taste.
3. Mix in tomato, onion, and chiles. Let stand for an hour before serving to allow flavors to blend.

CEVICHE

Beautiful to look at and elegant to serve, ceviche is ideal as a first course or in larger portions as an entree. The citric acid in the lime juice "cooks" the seafood. For a Guaymas touch, serve ceviche in sea shells.

Serves: 8 as an appetizer
4 as an entree

1¼ pounds fresh bay scallops, shrimp, or cod fish cut into
   1½-inch pieces, or any combination
Juice of 5 or 6 limes
3 or 4 fresh green chiles, parched and peeled (page 13),
   chopped
¼ cup olive oil
1 tablespoon chopped fresh cilantro
⅛ teaspoon ground Mexican oregano
Salt and freshly ground black pepper
1 avocado, ripe but firm, peeled and cut into thin wedges
¾ cup thinly sliced red Spanish onion; or 4 whole scallions,
   quartered lengthwise and cut into 1½-inch pieces
1 red ripe tomato, cut in wedges

1. Place seafood in a shallow glass dish and pour lime juice over. Marinate in refrigerator for 4 hours, turning occasionally.

2. Combine chiles, olive oil, cilantro, oregano and salt and pepper to taste. Pour over lime juice and seafood mixture and mix gently.

3. Add avocado wedges, onion or scallions, and tomato wedges. Stir very gently to coat with marinade, being careful not to break avocado or tomato wedges.

4. Chill 1 to 2 hours more and serve on a bed of lettuce.

TAQUITOS CON GUACAMOLE

These smaller versions of flautas ("flutes") are served with guacamole for dipping. A delightful appetizer.

Can be frozen in a rigid, sealed container uncooked for 2 months, cooked for 4 months. To serve cooked taquitos, heat on a baking sheet in a 425°F oven until hot, about 5 minutes.

Yield: 24

24 small corn tortillas
1½ cups (approximately) cooked meat filling such as beef,
  pork, or chicken (see fillings for tacos)
Lard for frying

1. Soften tortillas by placing each one briefly on a hot griddle or by wrapping in foil and heating for 15 minutes in oven.

2. Working on one taquito at a time, place a narrow pile of filling along the center of a tortilla; roll tightly and secure with a wooden pick.

3. Heat about ¼ inch of lard to medium heat in a large, heavy skillet. Fry the taquitos, turning to brown evenly. Drain well on paper towelling and serve with guacamole.

CARNITAS

Simple and delicious, these pieces of crisp, browned pork are served with a fresh salsa for dipping.

They can be frozen, tightly wrapped, for up to 2 months.

Yield: 6 to 8 servings

1½ pounds fresh pork, with fat and/or rind left on
2 cloves garlic, finely minced
½ teaspoon salt
1 teaspoon pure ground hot chile
Water

1. Cut the meat in bite-size cubes or in strips about 1 inch by 2½ inches.

2. Place meat in a heavy skillet; add garlic, salt, and chile and about ½ inch of water. Bring to a boil; then reduce heat and simmer, stirring from time to time, until all the water has evaporated.

3. Raise the heat a little and cook the meat until it is well browned and crisp. Serve warm.

NOTE: Any cut of pork will suffice; it is not necessary to use an expensive cut. The fat is left on because it fries crisp and has wonderful flavor and texture. You can prepare the meat ahead and warm the pieces on a baking sheet just prior to serving.

BEEF JERKY

As a mid-afternoon snack or a cocktail tidbit, Beef Jerky is delicious. Originally, the chile was added to the "jerked" beef to prolong freshness while the meat dried hung from high branches. This dried chile meat, when reconstituted, was probably this country's original convenience food.

Flank steak, excess fat removed and sliced about ⅛-inch
   thick, with the grain of the meat (or use "jerked" beef or
   vension)
1 clove garlic, well mashed
½ teaspoon salt
1 teaspoon pure ground red chile
¼ cup dry red wine
2 tablespoons wine vinegar

1. Place meat in a bowl. Make marinade of remaining ingredients and pour over meat; stir to coat. Marinate for 1 hour. Gently squeeze excess marinade off each piece of meat.

2. Lay each slice of meat across oven rack. Bake at 150°F for 6 hours. Store in an airtight container.

CHILE CON QUESO

The Southwest's most popular hot fonduelike dip; it is traditionally served with tostadas.

Chile Con Queso may be stored in a rigid container and frozen for up to 4 months.

Yield: 2 cups

⅓ cup vegetable oil
½ cup finely chopped onion, or 3 scallions with tops, chopped
1 clove garlic, finely minced
1 tablespoon flour·
¾ cup evaporated milk
1 fresh medium-size tomato, chopped
1 pound processed cheese food, cut into 1-inch cubes
¼ cup sharp Cheddar cheese, grated
¼ cup Monterey Jack cheese, grated
3 tablespoons finely minced jalapeño chiles (and juice to taste)

1. Heat oil in a heavy saucepan. Add onions and garlic and sauté until onions are translucent, about 3 to 5 minutes. Stir in flour.

2. Gradually add evaporated milk and cook until mixture thickens slightly.

3. Add tomato, cheeses, jalapeños, and juice. Cook and stir until thick and smooth, about 5 minutes.

4. Serve warm with tortilla chips.

NOTE: Keep warm in a chafing dish over steam. Leftover Chile Con Queso is excellent spooned over tostadas for instant nachos, over hamburgers or used in omelets.

CHILE QUESADILLAS

These small turnovers are a favorite Mexican snack. They are simply wheat tortillas stuffed with numerous combinations of fillings, folded over and fried until golden brown and crisp.

Yield: 24

> 6 wheat tortillas (8-inch size)
> 10 ounces Monterey Jack cheese, shredded
> 12 green chiles, parched and peeled (page 13), or 1 can (15 ounces) green chiles
> Lard for frying

1. Wrap tortillas in foil and heat in oven for 15 minutes to soften.

2. Prepare one at a time by placing a ½-inch layer of cheese on half of the tortilla; top with a single layer of green chiles. Fold tortilla in half and press the edges together. Turn the edges slightly and press firmly to secure; crimp the edges or press with the tines of a fork. To prevent uncooked quesadillas from drying out, cover with a cloth until all are prepared.

3. Bring about ¼ inch to ½ inch of lard to medium heat in a large, heavy skillet and fry the quesadillas until golden, turning once. Drain on paper towelling. Serve hot, cutting each into six wedge-shaped pieces.

Other fillings for quesadillas:

> crumbled and browned chorizo, red or green salsa, grated cheese
> pinto beans and jalapeño chiles
> beef or chicken fillings with a sprinkle of grated cheese or sour cream
> crabmeat, green chile, and sour cream

These tidbits can be frozen, individually wrapped, for up to 2 months. Reheat by placing on a baking sheet and baking at 400°F for 15 minutes.

CHILE-CHORIZO EMPANADAS

Empanadas have been enjoyed for centuries throughout the Spanish-speaking world. In fact, in the twelfth century cathedral of Santiago de Compostela, Spain, there is a statue of a man eating an empanada. Use any spicy mixture for these flavorful, versatile snacks—leftover bits of beef, cheese, chile, and taco fillings make terrific fillings.

Empanadas can be frozen for up to 2 months unbaked and for up to 4 months baked. Freeze in layers on wax paper, wrapped tightly in foil. Reheat at 400°F for 15 minutes.

Yield: about 24

½ pound chorizo sausage
2 to 4 tablespoons chopped green chile
⅓ cup sour cream, approximately
Pastry for a 9-inch, 2-crust pie

1. Crumble the sausage, brown it well in a skillet, and drain thoroughly. Add green chile to taste and enough sour cream to make a thick filling that holds together.
2. Preheat oven to 400°F. On a floured board, roll out the pastry and, using a 4-inch cutter, cut into rounds.
3. Spoon a little filling in the center of each pastry round, fold in half, moisten the edges with a drop of water, and seal with a fluted or forked edging.
4. Place empanadas on a baking sheet and bake for 15 minutes, or until golden.

Beverages

The spicy, hearty flavors of Southwestern foods need strong, flavored drinks. Rum drinks, beer, tequila, and heady, fruity wines such as zinfandel are popular beverages.

Tequila, Mexico's own creation and its most popular drink, plays an important part in drinks like the famed margarita, tequila sunrise, and tequila sour. Experienced drinkers take it by the shot with fresh lime and salt. Hold the lime between your thumb and index finger, place a pinch of salt on your moistened knuckle, and, with a sip of tequila, take a lick of salt and a suck of lime. Frozen rum daiquiris, plain or fruit-flavored, are a pleasantly refreshing hot weather drink. Fruity margaritas are also popular.

Kahlúa, a coffee-flavored liqueur from Mexico, is used in drinks as well as in many dessert recipes.

Salud!

MARGARITAS

Mexico's favorite cocktail, margaritas are best when made with freshly squeezed lime juice.

Yield: 4 drinks

Coarse or kosher salt
Juice of 4 or 5 limes (to measure 2 ounces)
2 ounces triple sec
6 ounces tequila
Ice
Egg white, optional (see variation below)

1. Place the salt in a small, dry saucer. About an hour before serving, squeeze the limes; then rub the top of each of four goblets to moisten; then dip each into the salt to generously coat the rims. Place glasses in freezer to frost.

2. Combine lime juice, triple sec, tequila, and ice. Blend in electric blender or shake well. Taste and add more lime juice or triple sec, if desired.

3. Pour into the frosted goblets and serve.

VARIATIONS: 1) For an extra frothy margarita, place ingredients in the blender with one egg white and blend until frothy. 2) I often combine fresh lemon juice and lime juice for a delicious, if unconventional, margarita.

STRAWBERRY MARGARITAS

Yield: 4 drinks

Juice of 4 or 5 limes (to measure 2 ounces)
4 ounces frozen strawberries
1 ounce triple sec
6 ounces tequila
3 cups ice cubes (or more)

1. Place all ingredients in a blender and blend until slushy. Serve in salt-rimmed goblets.

VARIATIONS: Peaches, bananas, or apricots may be substituted for strawberries.

"POOR MAN'S MARGARITA"

Begin with ice cold beer, not tequila!

Fresh limes
Coarse or kosher salt
Canned beer

1. Rub a piece of lime around the rims of beer cans to wet them; then rub the salt around generously. Place wedges of lime and a dish of salt in the middle of the table for those who wish more. Drink from the can for a true Guadalajara effect.

TEQUILA SOUR

Yield: 1 drink

Juice of ½ lemon
3 ounces tequila
2 teaspoons sugar
Ice
Half an orange slice and a maraschino cherry

1. Combine the first 4 ingredients in a shaker; shake well and pour into a glass.
2. Garnish with half an orange slice and a maraschino cherry.

TEQUILA SUNRISE

Slightly pink, pretty, and delicious.

Yield: 1 drink

Juice and rind of ½ lime
2 ounces tequila
1½ teaspoons grenadine syrup
⅓ cup orange juice

1. Place all ingredients in a glass filled with ice.
2. Stir thoroughly and serve.

BLOODY MARIA

This tequila Bloody Mary adds an authentic touch when served before a southwestern brunch.

Yield: 1 drink

⅔ cup tomato juice
2 ounces tequila
1 teaspoon Worcestershire sauce
Dash of celery salt
Few drops of hot pepper sauce
1 wedge of lime
Long strip of cucumber or celery

1. Salt the rim of a large, stemmed wine glass, using the procedure in the Margarita recipe (page 36).
2. Combine tomato juice, tequila, Worcestershire sauce, celery salt, and hot pepper sauce; pour into ice-filled glass.
3. Garnish with lime wedge and cucumber or celery strip.

NOTE: For an extra kick, squeeze fresh lime juice over the wedge of cucumber; then lightly sprinkle with coarse kosher salt and caribe chile.

FROZEN DAIQUIRIS

They have fabulous flavor and are *so* easy to make. These are my favorite daiquiris.

Yield: 4 drinks

1 cup light rum
4 ounces frozen limeade concentrate
8 to 10 ice cubes
4 thin slices lime

1. Place rum, limeade concentrate, and ice cubes in blender container.
2. Blend until a slushy consistency is achieved, adding a little more ice if necessary.
3. Pour into glasses, garnish with lime slices, and serve immediately.

NOTE: If a blender is not available, crush the ice cubes and shake well with the rum and limeade.

FROZEN FIESTA FRUIT DAIQUIRIS

Wonderfully easy to make and just as easy to sip. Plan to make
seconds for you and your guests.

Yield: 4 drinks

½ of a 6-ounce can of frozen limeade concentrate
2 medium-size ripe peaches, peeled
1 cup light rum
8 to 10 ice cubes

1. Place all ingredients in a blender container and blend until
mixture is slushy, adding more ice cubes if necessary.
2. Pour into chilled long-stemmed goblets or old-fashioned
glasses and serve immediately.

VARIATION: You can substitute 3 fresh apricots, ½ cup sweetened strawberries, 1 banana, or ½ cup fresh pineapple chunks for
the peaches; you may use frozen or well-drained canned fruit if
fresh fruit is unavailable.

"SMITH AND CURRANS"

When I recently visited Oklahoma, I first tasted this marvelous after-dinner drink; it comes directly from an oil rig crew.

Yield: 1 drink

Crushed ice
1 shot crème de cacao
1 shot milk
Club soda

1. Fill a tall glass with crushed ice.
2. Add the crème de cacao and milk. Fill the glass with club soda, stir, and serve.

ANGEL'S KISS

A smooth and creamy after-dinner drink.

Yield: 1 drink

1½ ounces kahlúa
Heavy cream (about ½ ounce)

1. Pour kahlúa into a liqueur glass.
2. Gently and slowly pour heavy cream on top to make a ¼-inch layer. Do not stir—the kahlúa and cream will remain in 2 layers.

NOTE: This drink is also very good over ice.

BLACK RUSSIAN

When making this drink, use Mexico's most famous liqueur—
kahlúa. The Black Russian is an all-time favorite after-dinner
drink or cocktail.

Yield: 1 drink

1 óunce kahlúa
3 ounces vodka
Ice cubes

1. Pour kahlúa and vodka over ice in an old-fashioned glass.
2. Stir and serve.

SANGRIA

Yield: about 2 quarts

1 lime
1 orange
1 lemon
1 banana
⅔ cup water
1 cup sugar
1 stick cinnamon (about 3 inches long)
Ice
2 fifths dry red wine (or a 1.5 liter bottle)

1. Slice the lime, orange, lemon, and banana and place in a bowl.

2. Place the water, sugar, and cinnamon stick in a saucepan and bring to a boil to dissolve sugar. Pour hot syrup over the fruit and chill thoroughly.

3. Put ice in a punch bowl or large pitcher, pour in the chilled fruit in syrup, and then add the wine.

4. Stir and serve.

BLONDE SANGRIA

Yield: about 2 quarts

²/₃ cup water
³/₄ cup sugar
1 apple
1 lemon
1 orange
1 pint fresh whole strawberries, rinsed, stems removed
Ice
2 fifths dry white wine (or a 1.5 liter bottle)
Few sprigs of fresh mint

1. Place water and sugar in a small saucepan and bring to a boil to dissolve sugar. Cool.

2. Slice the apple, lemon, and orange and place in a bowl with the strawberries. Pour the cooled syrup over and chill thoroughly.

3. Put ice in a large pitcher or punch bowl, add the fruit in syrup, and then add the wine. Stir.

4. Garnish with mint and serve.

TEXAS PUNCH

Deliciously refreshing for warm weather entertaining, this punch is versatile enough to meet the demands of changing supplies in your liquor cabinet.

Yield: 1¹/₂ gallons

2 or 3 trays of ice
2 bottles (28 ounces each) lemon-lime carbonated beverage
6 ounces frozen limeade concentrate
12 ounces frozen lemonade concentrate
1 quart light rum
1 pint brandy (or dark rum)
1 bottle (28 ounces) club soda
1 lemon, thinly sliced
1 lime, thinly sliced

1. Place ice in a large punch bowl. Add all liquid ingredients; stir to blend.
2. Add lemon and lime slices for garnish and serve.

VARIATIONS: If desired, vodka or gin may be substituted for the rums. Orange juice or pineapple juice may be substituted for the limeade and lemonade.

NEW MEXICAN CHOCOLATE

A deliciously spiced hot chocolate, very similar to that made with
Mexican chocolate.

Yield: 6 drinks

¼ cup plus 2 tablespoons sugar
1 tablespoon flour
¼ cup cocoa powder
Dash of salt
½ teaspoon ground cinnamon
¼ teaspoon ground cloves
¾ cup cold water
3 cups milk
1½ teaspoons vanilla extract
Whipped cream
6 cinnamon sticks

1. In a saucepan, combine the sugar, flour, cocoa, salt, and
spices. Add the ¾ cup water, bring to a boil, and then simmer for
3 minutes.

2. Gradually add the milk and heat to scalding—do not boil.
Using a molinello (a Mexican chocolate stirrer), a fork, or a
rotary beater, whip the chocolate.

3. Pour hot chocolate into mugs or stemmed glasses and serve
immediately, garnished with a dollop of whipped cream and a
cinnamon stick stirrer.

MEXICAN COFFEE

1. For each eight cups of coffee, add ³/₄ teaspoon ground cinnamon to the top of the ground coffee, then brew coffee as usual. Or place a cinnamon stick in the pot with the water and then brew the coffee.

NOTE: Be certain to make a rich, dark pot of coffee. Many people like to serve *piloncillo* with the coffee or to add about ¹/₃ cup to the pot before serving. Piloncillo is unrefined sugar. It is golden in color, and has a more caramel flavor than white sugar. Brown sugar may be substituted if *piloncillo* is unavailable.

Salsas (Sauces)

A southwestern meal would be incomplete without a bowl of salsa (Spanish for sauce). Salsa may be green or red or even have a creamy base; it may be fresh or cooked, hot or mild. The sauces in this chapter can be adapted for a variety of uses and are included in many recipes throughout this book.

Relish-type salsas are often served as table sauces for dunking tostadas. But salsas are not only served as condiments; they are the essence of many Tex-Mex dishes such as enchiladas and tamales.

If you're not sure what type of sauce to serve with a particular dish, you can use the same general rule that applies to choosing wine: red salsas with red meats and green salsas with light meats, such as pork, veal, poultry, and fish.

I've also included some recipes for preserves and relishes in this chapter. These delicacies are another special attraction of the Southwestern dinner table. I'm particularly fond of jalapeño jelly—its unique sweet and snappy flavor goes fabulously with grilled meats or with mild cheeses as an hors d'oeuvre.

SALSA FRESCA I
(SALSA CRUDA OR FRESH CHILE SAUCE)

This refreshing sauce can be as mild or as hot as you like, depending on the chiles used. I first learned of this simple sauce in the late fifties, when it was featured at the Shed Restaurant in Santa Fe. It was served atop freshly broiled hamburgers, which were served on tarragon-basil buttered English muffins. Absolutely heavenly! Any leftovers of this sauce can be added to guacamole or chile con queso, and can be frozen for up to 4 months for later use in cooked dishes.

Yield: 1 1/2 to 2 cups

1 large fresh tomato, finely chopped
1/2 cup finely chopped onion, or 2 scallions with tops included
4 green chiles, parched and peeled (page 13) chopped, or 4 ounces of canned chopped green chiles
1 clove garlic, finely minced
1/2 teaspoon salt

1. Combine all ingredients; allow to marinate for at least 15 minutes. Sauce keeps for 1 week when refrigerated.

SALSA FRESCA II

My all-time favorite fresh sauce. Serve as a table sauce or over tacos or tostadas . . . I guarantee that absolutely all foods you serve with this salsa will be even better than you ever thought possible.

Yield: about 2 cups

1⅓ cups drained, canned tomatoes
¼ cup fresh tomato, finely diced
4 teaspoons red wine vinegar
1 teaspoon finely chopped onion
4 teaspoons freshly squeezed lime juice
1 teaspoon finely chopped parsley
¼ teaspoon salt
1 small clove garlic, crushed
1 tablespoon water
2 teaspoons jalapeño juice
2 teaspoons snipped chives
1½ tablespoons chopped green chiles
½ teaspoon finely chopped serrano chile
¼ cup chopped green bell pepper
Pinch each of ground Mexican oregano, ground comino,
    sugar

1. Chop canned tomatoes and place in a bowl. Add all other ingredients and stir well to combine.
2. Refrigerate overnight in a covered container to allow flavors to blend.

RED CHILE SAUCE

Essential for many Southwestern recipes, this sauce is served over a multitude of main dishes, such as enchiladas, burritos, and chiles rellenos. Pure ground New Mexican chile is the key ingredient; the flavor of the sauce can be adjusted by using ground chile of varying degrees of hotness. Sometimes thought of as a tomato-based sauce, it is not; the color comes solely from the chile.

This sauce can be frozen for up to 8 months. I'd suggest freezing it in ½-cup portions.

Yield: about 2½ cups

2 tablespoons lard or bacon drippings
2 tablespoons flour
¼ cup pure ground red chile (mild or hot or in combination)
2 cups cooled beef bouillon or water
¾ teaspoon salt
1 clove garlic, crushed
Pinch of ground Mexican oregano
Pinch of ground comino (cumin)

1. Melt lard over low heat in a saucepan. Add the flour and stir until well blended and slightly golden.
2. Remove pan from heat and completely stir in the chile. Return to heat, and, stirring constantly, add the bouillon or water. Add seasonings and cook and stir for about 10 minutes. Add hot ground chile to taste if a hotter flavor is desired. It is important to begin with a milder chile if you are making this sauce for the first time or if you are using a new type of chile—you can always make it hotter but you can't take the heat out!
3. Simmer for at least 5 more minutes to develop the flavor.

VARIATION: Sauté ½ pound of beef, cut in very small cubes or coarsely ground, omit the lard, and proceed with the rest of the recipe. This meaty sauce is great for enchiladas.

SALSA CARIBE

Northern New Mexico or Chimayo chiles are traditionally used to prepare this salsa. Many aficionados prefer the sweet, hot flavor of this sauce.

1. Place ¼ cup crushed mild red chiles (about 6 to 8 whole chiles) in a thin layer in a shallow pan and roast them at 300°F for 15 minutes, or until the color darkens.

2. Combine roasted chile with 1 cup water and simmer, covered, for 30 minutes. Strain and discard the skins and seeds.

3. Prepare Red Chile Sauce recipe using this caribe liquid in place of the ¼ cup ground chile, and reduce the bouillon by ¾ cup.

SALSA COLORADO (HOT RED SAUCE)

Hot and terrific! I first sampled this sauce at a very successful Santa Fe restaurant, and, when the owners wouldn't part with the recipe, I went home and tested, tasted, and tested again. I think I may have discovered their secret! This salsa does not freeze well but will keep for several weeks in the refrigerator.

Yield: ³/₄ cup

³/₄ cup fresh or whole canned tomatoes, crushed
1½ teaspoons (or more) chile pequín, finely crushed
1½ teaspoons freshly squeezed lime juice
1½ teaspoons cider vinegar
Pinch of ground Mexican oregano
1 clove garlic, crushed
³/₄ teaspoon ground comino
½ teaspoon minced fresh cilantro, or ground dried coriander (optional)

1. Place all ingredients in a covered jar. Shake until thoroughly mixed.

GREEN CHILE SAUCE

A basic! Great with chicken and seafood. It can be frozen for up to 8 months.

Yield: 2 cups

1 tablespoon lard, bacon fat, or butter
2/3 cup chopped onion
2 tablespoons flour
1½ cups chicken broth or 2 cups canned, stewed tomatoes
1 cup (or more) chopped green chiles
1 large clove garlic, finely minced
¾ teaspoon salt
Dash of ground comino (cumin)

1. Melt the lard in a saucepan over medium heat. Sauté the onion until soft. Stir in the flour.

2. Add the broth or tomatoes. Then add chiles, garlic, salt, and comino.

3. Simmer for 20 minutes; serve as desired. To use in enchiladas, see Green Chile Enchiladas (page 121–22).

SALSA VERDE (MEXICAN-STYLE RELISH)

An old Mexican favorite that is good over almost any meat or tortilla dish. Tomatillos, available in Mexican specialty shops, should always be used. Don't substitute unripe green tomatoes because they lack the subtle, sweet taste of the tomatillo.

This salsa can be frozen for 4 months.

Yield: about 2 cups

⅔ cup onion, finely minced
1 tablespoon minced fresh cilantro, optional
1 jalapeño or serrano chile, finely minced
½ teaspoon salt, optional
1 can (13 ounces) tomatillos, drained.

1. Blend all the ingredients in an electric blender or food processor. (If no blender or food processor is available, use a fork or mortar and pestle to thoroughly mash the ingredients.)
2. Taste, and, if necessary, adjust seasonings.

AVOCADO SAUCE

A simple, refreshing sauce that is a perfect topping for grilled meats and poultry. If you happen to have guacamole on hand, thin it with olive oil and jalapeño juice for a quick substitute.

Yield: approximately 2 cups

3 tablespoons olive oil
1 teaspoon finely minced jalapeño chile, or to taste
1 tablespoon wine vinegar (or a dash of jalapeño juice to taste)
½ teaspoon salt
¼ teaspoon freshly ground pepper
2 teaspoons minced parsley
1 teaspoon fresh minced cilantro, optional
1 large ripe avocado, peeled and diced
1 medium-size tomato, seeds squeezed out, finely chopped
3 tablespoons thinly sliced scallions

1. Put first seven ingredients in a small jar. Cover and shake well until thoroughly mixed.

2. Put diced avocado, tomato, and scallions in a serving bowl. Pour dressing over, stir gently to combine, and let stand about 15 minutes, until flavors blend.

SALSA RANCHERO

Delicious and picante—use on huevos rancheros, fish burritos, or chicken enchiladas.

Pack in ½- or ¾-cup portions and freeze for up to 8 months.

Yield: approximately 2 cups

> 1 tablespoon vegetable oil
> ⅔ cup chopped onion
> 1½ tablespoons minced serrano (or other hot green) chile
> 2 medium-size tomatoes, peeled and chopped
> ½ cup tomato juice
> ½ teaspoon salt

1. Heat oil in saucepan. Add onion and chile, and sauté until onion is soft and translucent.

2. Add chopped tomatoes, juice, and salt. Reduce heat and simmer for 5 minutes.

3. Serve hot.

CREAMY SALSA

This sauce is great on Spiced Chicken Tacos (page 90).

Yield: 1¹/₄ cups

1/2 cup sour cream
1/2 cup mayonnaise
1/4 cup Salsa Verde (see page 56)
1 teaspoon salt
1 tablespoon lime juice or lemon juice
1/2 teaspoon minced serrano chile (or to taste)
1/2 teaspoon caribe (crushed red Northern New Mexico chile)

1. Combine all ingredients except caribe and chill thoroughly. Sprinkle caribe over salsa just prior to serving.

"MAGIC SAUCE"

The "magic" of this chile sauce is in its ingredients, which include chocolate and cinnamon. You'll love it over any beef-filled Southwest tortilla dish such as burritos, enchiladas, and tamales. It can be frozen for up to 8 months.

Yield: 2 cups

2 cups Red Chile Sauce (see page 52)
1/4 square unsweetened chocolate
1 1/2 teaspoons light brown sugar
Pinch of ground cloves
Pinch of allspice
1/8 teaspoon cinnamon
1/2 teaspoon wine vinegar
1 teaspoon ground almonds
1 teaspoon dark raisins
1/16 teaspoon ground coriander

1. Combine all ingredients in a medium-size saucepan.
2. Simmer over low heat, stirring constantly until chocolate is melted and flavors blend, about 20 minutes.

MOLE SAUCE—SPICY TOMATO AND CHOCOLATE SAUCE

A rich, delicious sauce for chicken and other poultry. Simmer cooked chicken pieces in the sauce or use the sauce with chicken-filled or turkey-filled tamales, burritos, or chimichangos. You can pack in 1- to 1½-cup quantities and freeze for up to 8 months.

Yield: about 2³⁄₄ cups

2-day-old, air-dried corn tortillas
2 tablespoons seedless raisins
½ square (½ ounce) unsweetened chocolate
¼ cup blanched almonds
1 small onion, chopped
1 medium-size green pepper, coarsely chopped
1 large fresh tomato, quartered
1 clove garlic
3 tablespoons flour
1 tablespoon ground pure hot red chile
¼ teaspoon ground cinnamon
¼ teaspoon ground cloves
2½ cups chicken stock

1. Grind tortillas, raisins, chocolate, almonds, onion, green pepper, tomato, and garlic in a food processor or electric blender. Place mixture in a medium-size saucepan.
2. Stir in flour and spices. Add the 2½ cups chicken stock and stir until well blended. Bring mixture to a boil, reduce heat and simmer, uncovered, for about 20 minutes, stirring occasionally. Sauce should be of medium consistency—a little thicker than heavy cream. If necessary, thin with a bit more chicken stock.

Sopas (Soups) and Stews

The Spaniards arrived on the shores of the New World bearing such unheard-of gifts as chickens, rice, cattle, sheep, wheat, almonds—and sopas, or soups. Soups had not been a part of the Indian kitchen, but they were readily adopted by the Indians who created countless variations by combining native New World with European ingredients. Although served for hundreds of years in Mexico, sopas are a relatively new course in southwestern cooking and are now quickly increasing in popularity.

In Mexico, there are two basic types of sopas—wet and dry. The wet sopas are what we know as soups, either broth-based or cream-based. The dry soups, or sopa secas, have a heavy, starchy base of tortillas, hominy, rice or other grains. They are traditionally served after the wet soup as a separate course, and are an excellent accompaniment to a main course in lieu of potatoes, rice, or beans. The origin of sopa secas is not clear, but a reasonable assumption is that they may have been created from a need to make a filling meal from whatever was available.

SOPA DE AJO (GARLIC SOUP)

One of the most frequently requested recipes by travelers returning from Old Mexico. It can be frozen in an airtight container for up to 3 months.

> 2 tablespoons olive oil
> 1 small onion, very finely minced
> 5 cloves garlic, very finely minced or mashed with a mortar and pestle
> 4½ cups rich chicken broth or bouillon
> 1 bay leaf
> 1 teaspoon fresh cilantro, very finely minced (or substitute fresh parsley)
> ½ teaspoon salt
> Freshly ground pepper
> 1 slice white bread, crumbled into fine crumbs or ¼ cup crumbled tostadas or tortillas
> 1 egg yolk, well beaten
> ½ cup light cream
> Croutons

1. Heat olive oil in a large saucepan. Sauté onion and garlic until onion is soft. Stir in 2 cups broth, the bay leaf, cilantro, salt, pepper, and bread crumbs. Bring to a boil, reduce heat, cover, and simmer for 30 minutes.

2. Add the remaining 2½ cups broth. Mix 1 cup of the soup into the beaten egg yolk, and then return all to the pan. Heat, without boiling; add the ½ cup cream. Taste and adjust seasonings.

3. Place soup in serving bowls, garnish with croutons, and serve immediately.

SOUTHWESTERN ZUCCHINI SOUP

Smooth and spicy delight. Seal in airtight container and freeze for up to 3 months.

Yield: 4 servings

4 tablespoons butter
1 large onion, chopped
1 clove garlic, minced
4 zucchini squash, medium-size (about 8 inches in length), sliced
1 teaspoon pure ground mild red chile
¼ teaspoon pure ground hot red chile
¼ teaspoon ground Mexican oregano
½ teaspoon salt
1⅔ cup chicken broth, fresh or canned
½ cup light cream

1. Melt butter in a heavy skillet; add onion, garlic, and squash; sauté until tender.
2. Transfer mixture to blender or food processor and add broth. Process until smooth.
3. Put mixture in a saucepan and heat. Add cream and simmer for 5 minutes without boiling.
4. Place in bowls, garnish with a light sprinkling of ground chile, and serve.

NOTE: If a very spicy soup is desired, add more hot ground chile to taste.

BLACK BEAN SOUP

Inspired by the Brazilian national dish, feijoada, this hearty soup is substantial enough to serve as a main dish. It can be frozen in an airtight container for up to 4 months.

Yield: 6 servings

4 cups water
2 cups dry black beans, washed and picked over
3 cloves garlic, minced
1 large onion, chopped
1 large stalk celery, chopped
1 tomato, peeled and chopped
1 pork or ham bone
1½ teaspoons salt
Freshly ground black pepper
½ teaspoon dry mustard
1½ teaspoons (or more) pure ground mild chile
3 tablespoons dry sherry
Sour cream
Scallions, sliced

1. In a large pot, bring 4 cups water and the beans to a boil. Simmer for 10 minutes, cover, and let sit for an hour.

2. Add garlic, onion, celery, tomato, and pork or ham bone, and simmer until beans are very tender, about 2 to 3 hours, adding more water as it evaporates.

3. Remove the bone and put soup in a blender, 2 cups at a time, blending until smooth. Return to the pot. Add remaining ingredients except sour cream and scallions; taste and adjust the seasonings. Reheat without boiling.

4. Serve in soup bowls garnished with a dollop of sour cream and a sprinkling of sliced scallions.

VARIATION: For a more continental accent, serve laced with additional sherry or rum, before adding sour cream and scallions.

CHICKEN SOUP WITH GARBANZOS AND CHILES

The inspiration for this sopa came from the terrific soups served in the sleepy, quaint villages dotting the northern Mexico mountains. This is a wonderful main dish soup-stew. Serve with hot, soft tortillas. This sopa can be frozen for up to 3 months. Prepare to step 3. Add the cheese and avocado after reheating the soup.

Yield: 6 servings

1 whole chicken (3½ to 4 pounds)
6 cups water
1 carrot, cut in 1-inch pieces
1 clove garlic, crushed
2 bay leaves
7 whole peppercorns
Salt
6 green chiles, parched and peeled (page 13), cut in thin
   strips
2 cans (16 ounces each) garbanzos (chick peas), drained
4 scallions, tops included, cut in 1-inch pieces
1 cup cubed Monterey Jack cheese
1 avocado, peeled and pitted, sliced into thin wedges

1. Place the chicken in a large pot or Dutch oven. Add water, carrot, onion, garlic, bay leaves, peppercorns, and salt to taste. Bring to a boil, cover, and simmer until chicken is tender, about 1 hour. Remove and drain the chicken. Strain the broth and return broth to the pot.

2. Boil broth for about 15 minutes to reduce slightly. Add the green chiles and garbanzos; simmer for 5 minutes. Taste and adjust seasonings.

3. Cut the chicken into serving pieces. Add chicken to the pot; simmer 5 minutes, and then add the scallions and simmer 5 minutes longer (the scallions should remain fairly firm).

4. Add the cheese cubes and immediately serve the soup garnished with avocado slices. The cheese cubes should be soft but still intact when soup is served.

GAZPACHO

Served icy cold, gazpacho is an unequaled way to begin a meal or refresh the palate after a spicy main course. Light and refreshing, it makes an excellent summer luncheon meal when served with a hearty taco or tostado-type salad. It must be served fresh.

Yield: 6 servings

1½ cups tomato juice
1 clove garlic, crushed
2 tablespoons wine vinegar
3 tablespoons olive oil
½ teaspoon salt
¼ teaspoon freshly ground black pepper
1 teaspoon minced fresh cilantro or parsley
1 large cucumber, peeled, seeded, and chopped
1 medium-size onion, chopped
3 large ripe tomatoes, peeled, seeded, and chopped
1 green bell pepper (or green chile if you prefer), seeded and chopped
Romaine lettuce leaves
6 crusty slices bread, cut 1-inch thick

1. Place tomato juice, garlic, vinegar, oil, salt, pepper, and cilantro or parsley in blender or food processor container. Process briefly until well blended.

2. Add the cucumber, onion, tomato, and bell pepper or chile and process until smooth. *Or,* if more texture is desired, chop these ingredients very fine and stir them into the soup. Taste and adjust seasonings.

3. Chill for at least 2 hours and serve in small bowls, goblets, or glasses lined with romaine lettuce leaves with a slice of bread in the bottom of each. Garnish with a sprinkling of additional minced cilantro or parsley.

CHILAQUILES

This dish is an excellent way to recycle leftover taco shells or fried tortillas for enchiladas.

Yield: 4 to 6 servings

Lard or oil for frying
12 corn tortillas
3 green chiles (or more to taste), finely chopped
3 large ripe tomatoes, cut into thin wedges
1 medium-size onion, chopped
1 clove garlic, very finely minced
1/8 teaspoon ground comino
1/4 teaspoon salt
Freshly ground black pepper
Optional: 1 cup shredded Monterey Jack cheese, or 4 lightly
    fried eggs

1. Heat about 1/4 inch lard in a large, heavy skillet. Cut the tortillas in half and then in 3/4-inch strips. Fry briefly in the oil until almost crisp. (If previously fried, do not refry.)

2. Heat remaining ingredients in a large saucepan; simmer for about 5 minutes. Add the tortilla strips and simmer for no more than 5 minutes longer.

3. Spoon onto plates and serve immediately with a bit of shredded Monterey Jack cheese on top, if desired. Or serve topped with a fried or poached egg for a hearty breakfast or brunch.

SOPA DE TORTILLA (TORTILLA SOUP)

Great for lunch!

Yield: 2 to 4 servings

2 tablespoons bacon fat or lard
1 medium-size onion, chopped
1 clove garlic, minced
3 cups rich chicken broth or beef stock
½ cup tomato juice
3 whole dried Anaheim or other mild chiles, crushed (or ¼
 cup caribe chile)
¼ teaspoon ground comino
4 cups crisp tostadas (page 22)
½ cup grated Monterey Jack cheese

1. Heat bacon fat in a medium-size saucepan. Sauté the onion and garlic until onion is soft. Add the broth, tomato juice, chiles, and comino. Cover and simmer for 30 minutes.
2. Divide about half the tostadas among the soup bowls. Ladle the steaming hot soup over and sprinkle with grated cheese and a few more tostadas. Serve remaining tostadas separately.

NOTE: Stale tostadas can be warmed in the oven, then used.

Ensaladas (Salads)

Lettuce, tomato, onions, and guacamole—the basic southwestern salad ingredients—are used as a garnish for many regional main dishes. Cole slaw, guacamole, and pickled and marinated fresh vegetables very often play the role of salad in a dinner or luncheon.

Innovative main dish salads such as compuestas served in ruffly fried tortillas are relative newcomers to New Mexican cuisine. Each recipe can be adapted and expanded in many ways to suit your whim or fancy.

One of my favorite salads is a simple dish of sliced avocado, red ripe tomatoes, and Spanish onions seasoned with a bit of green chile and marinated in Vinaigrette Dressing (page 76).

TACO SALAD

An attractive, delicious, and filling buffet salad, this mixture has the crisp tortillas in the salad rather than the salad in the tortilla. For convenience in entertaining, prepare the meat topping ahead of time and reheat before assembling the salad.

Yield: 6 servings

Meat Topping:

1 pound lean ground beef
1 onion, chopped
1 clove garlic, minced
1 tablespoon pure ground mild red chile, or to taste
¼ teaspoon Mexican oregano
3 tablespoons red wine vinegar
3 tablespoons salad oil
½ cup water
2 cups cooked pinto beans, drained
Salt

Salad:

1½ quarts mixed salad greens, torn in bite-size pieces
1½ cups shredded Monterey Jack and Cheddar cheese
    combination
4 scallions, sliced
2 medium-size tomatoes, cut in wedges
1 avocado, peeled and pitted, cut into thin slices
⅓ cup sliced pitted black olives
8 ounces tostadas, or broken taco shells
Salsa (pages 49–61)

1. Brown the beef, onion, and garlic. Add the ground chile, oregano, vinegar, oil, water, beans, and salt to taste. Simmer for about 20 minutes to blend flavors.

2. To assemble the salad, place greens in a large salad bowl. Top with warm beef mixture, cheese, scallions, and tomatoes. Arrange avocado slices and black olives over. Coarsely crush a handful of tostadas and sprinkle on top.

3. Serve the remaining tostadas in a separate bowl and pass the salsa.

NOTE: This is a terrific way to salvage broken tostados and taco shells.

VARIATION: Place salad briefly in hot oven or under broiler to melt the cheese.

MARINATED COLESLAW

Great to keep on hand at all times. This slaw is a wonderful accompaniment to many Southwestern main dishes and is a delicious addition to burritos, tacos, and tostados. It's ideal to take along on picnics.

Yield: about 8 cups

> 1 pound cabbage, chopped or finely shredded (about ½ of a
>   medium-size head)
> ½ teaspoon salt
> ½ cup salad oil
> ½ cup white vinegar
> ½ cup sugar
> ¼ to ½ teaspoon caribe chile, optional

1. Place cabbage in a large bowl and season with salt.

2. Place the oil, vinegar, and sugar in a saucepan. Bring to a boil, stirring to dissolve sugar. Pour hot dressing over the cabbage and marinate at room temperature for at least an hour or in refrigerator for 3 hours. Stir in caribe chile, if desired, adding ¼ teaspoon—taste and add more to suit taste.

BEAN-STUFFED AVOCADOS

Very rich and hearty. All that's needed to complete a dinner is a meat dish.

Yield: 6 servings

1 can (16 ounces) chick peas, well drained
1 can (16 ounces) pinto beans or kidney beans, well drained
1 small onion, finely chopped
1 medium-size tomato, seeds gently squeezed out, chopped
½ cup salad oil or olive oil
¼ cup vinegar
1 or 2 teaspoons finely minced jalapeño chile, optional
2 teaspoons sugar
½ teaspoon salt
Freshly ground black pepper
3 avocados
Lettuce leaves

1. Place chick peas, beans, onion, and tomato in a bowl.
2. Combine oil, vinegar, jalapeño, sugar, salt, and black pepper. Pour over bean mixture and marinate in the refrigerator for several hours or overnight.
3. To assemble salads, cut the avocados in half and remove the pits. Place lettuce leaves on each plate, top with an avocado half, and spoon bean mixture over.

VARIATION: Add 1 cup cubed Monterey Jack cheese to the bean mixture. Serve bean salad in lettuce cups if avocados are not available.

ENSALADA DE CAMARONES (SHRIMP SALAD)

A refreshing and elegant salad. Garlic and chiles combine with shrimp and peas to make a delectably spiced first course or luncheon entree.

Yield: 4 servings

1½ pounds fresh shrimp, peeled and deveined
1 package (10 ounces) frozen peas, or 1½ cups fresh peas
1 scallion, very thinly sliced, tops included
2 tablespoons pimento, sliced in thin strips
¾ cup mayonnaise
1 clove garlic, thoroughly mashed
1 tablespoon minced cilantro (optional), or parsley
2 green chiles, parched and peeled (page 13), finely chopped,
   or ¼ cup canned chopped green chiles, or 1 canned
   jalapeño chile, very finely chopped
Lime wedges

1. Cook shrimp in boiling salted water for 3 or 4 minutes; drain and cool. Cook peas until tender but still slightly firm; drain and cool. Combine the shrimp and peas with the scallion and pimento. Chill thoroughly.

2. Mix together the mayonnaise, garlic, cilantro, and chile to taste. Gently combine with the chilled shrimp and peas.

3. Serve the shrimp salad on lettuce leaves or in avocado halves garnished with lime wedges. Warmed hard crusty bolillos (pages 198–99) or wheat tortillas are a delicious accompaniment.

POTATO AND GREEN BEAN SALAD

Serve with grilled meats, poultry, or fish.

Yield: 8 servings

1½ pounds potatoes (about 8 small or 5 medium-size)
1 pound fresh green beans
2 scallions, chopped, tops included
⅓ cup thinly sliced radishes
¼ cup chopped green chile (optional)
¾ cup Vinaigrette Dressing (recipe follows)

1. Peel potatoes and cut in long pieces, about ½ inch by 2½ inches. Steam until just tender, but not falling apart.
2. Rinse green beans and trim ends, leaving the beans whole. Steam until just tender.
3. Place hot potatoes and beans in a bowl. Sprinkle with the scallions, radishes, and green chile. Pour dressing over; stir gently to coat. Chill in refrigerator for at least 3 hours before serving.

Vinaigrette Dressing   *Yield: 2 cups*

1½ cups olive oil
½ cup wine vinegar (white or red)
1 clove garlic, crushed
1 teaspoon sugar
1 tablespoon tomato paste, optional
2 teaspoons dry mustard
½ teaspoon salt
¼ teaspoon ground Mexican oregano
¼ teaspoon freshly ground black pepper

1. Place all ingredients in a jar; cover and shake well to combine.

NEW MEXICAN CHICKEN SALAD

Yield: 4 servings

¾ cup uncooked rice
2 cups chicken broth
4 cups cooked chicken, well seasoned, cut in cubes
⅔ cup mayonnaise
½ cup cubed jalapēno Monterey Jack cheese
⅓ cup chopped green chile

1. Cook rice in chicken broth until fluffy; then cool.
2. Combine cooked rice and chicken in a bowl. Add remaining ingredients and mix. Taste and adjust seasonings, if desired.
3. Serve salad on a bed of lettuce garnished with avocado slices sprinkled with fresh lime juice and topped with a little chopped red ripe tomato.

GUACAMOLE AND CAULIFLOWER SALAD

Yield: 4 to 6 servings

1 medium-size head of cauliflower, broken into flowerettes
⅓ cup Vinaigrette Dressing (page 76) or your favorite vinegar
    and oil dressing
Lettuce leaves
1 recipe Guacamole (page 26), thinned slightly with a bit of
    cream

1. Steam the cauliflower until tender, but not soft; pour dressing over and chill.
2. Line a shallow serving bowl with lettuce leaves. Place cauliflower on top and spoon guacamole over. Serve.

CRABMEAT, SHRIMP, AND AVOCADO SALAD

A hot main dish salad and a very special treat.

Yield: 4 servings

1 cup cooked flaked crabmeat
1 cup cooked small shrimp
3 tablespoons minced scallions
1½ teaspoons lime juice
2 large avocados
½ cup heavy cream
⅓ cup milk
1½ teaspoons lime juice
½ teaspoon salt
1 teaspoon ground pure mild red chile (or use minced
    jalapēno chile or jalapēno chile juice to taste)
1 teaspoon minced cilantro, or 2 teaspoons minced parsley
4 large lettuce leaves
1 medium-size tomato, quartered
12 large black olives
4 lime wedges

1. Combine crabmeat, shrimp, and 2 tablespoons scallions. Sprinkle 1½ teaspoons lime juice over and place in oven at low temperature to warm.

2. Halve the avocados, remove the pits, and scoop out the pulp, leaving about ¼ inch inside shell. Save shells.

3. Place the avocado pulp, cream, milk, lime juice, salt, chile, and cilantro in blender container and process until smooth. Remove to a medium-size saucepan and heat gently—do not boil.

4. Add warmed crabmeat and shrimp; stir to combine.

5. Place a lettuce leaf on each of 4 plates and top with reserved avocado shells. Spoon warm seafood mixture into shells. Garnish with tomato wedges, black olives, lime wedges, and reserved scallions. Serve with steaming hot tortillas.

MUSHROOMS AND ONIONS EN ESCABECHE

Serve as a garnish for main dishes or as an hors d'oeuvre. Don't let the recipe limit your imagination—you can use crisp-cooked steamed cauliflower, broccoli, celery, carrots, green and red bell peppers, green beans, zucchini or yellow summer squash, chayote, and other vegetables that are delicious.

Yield: about 3 cups

¼ cup salad oil or olive oil
½ cup white wine vinegar
1 clove garlic, very finely minced
½ teaspoon salt
¼ teaspoon freshly ground black pepper
¼ teaspoon ground Mexican oregano
1 sprig celery leaves, chopped
2 medium-size onions, sliced and separated into rings
½ pound fresh mushrooms, washed and left whole

1. In a medium-size saucepan combine oil, vinegar, garlic, salt, pepper, oregano, and celery leaves. Bring to a boil, add onion rings, and simmer for 3 minutes.
2. Pour mixture over mushrooms and marinate in refrigerator for several hours or overnight. Serve at room temperature.

TORTILLAS/
SPECIALTIES

Tacos

Tacos have become popular in the United States and with little wonder—tacos are fun, easy to make, and very versatile. Crunchy, fried taco shells are a creation of the southwestern United States. In Old Mexico, warm, soft corn tortillas are used to contain varied fillings.

Tacos are often a first introduction to the joys of southwestern cooking. It's comforting to realize that, as a snack or meal, tacos are healthy—beans, meat, vegetables, and cheese inside a corn masa shell are very nutritious. And diet-conscious diners should know that a taco shell has only about 50 calories, fewer than 2 slices of bread!

Keep in mind that the very best taco shells are fresh and crisply fried just prior to using. The second choice is to use packaged taco shells and warm them in the oven before adding the fillings. For a New Mexico-style taco, turn the oven temperature up to 450°F and place the assembled tacos in the oven for 2 to 3 minutes to melt the cheese.

The crisp, folded tortilla shell holds an almost endless array of fillings topped with chopped tomato, shredded lettuce, and grated cheese. A spoonful or two of spicy salsa completes the taco. When filled with hearty meat/bean/rice combinations, allow 2 to 3 tacos per person as a main course.

Keep taco shells on hand at all times as a way to use leftovers on those "what to do for dinner" evenings, and keep in mind that tacos are great for entertaining (see "The Taco Bar," pages 96–97).

This chapter includes a large variety of taco recipes, and this is only the beginning. Many other recipes throughout the book make super tacos (one of my personal favorites is Carne Adobada (page 163), served with accompaniments of your choice). Or, use shrimp, crabmeat, lobster, leftover fish, etc. for seafood tacos topped with guacamole or Creamy Salsa (page 59). Also, warmed frijoles or frijoles refritos with cheese, lettuce, and Salsa Fresca (page 50) or Salsa Verde (page 56) are super when heaped into warmed taco shells. Just let your refrigerator and pantry be a starting point for more ingenious creations of your own!

CRISP-FRIED TACO SHELLS

The best taco shells are those freshly made. There's no special trick to frying them, although a deep-frying temperature of at least 375°F is essential. Just one or two practice shells will show you how long to fry them to firm, crisp, lightly golden perfection.

The shells can be frozen for up to 1 year. Stuff crumpled paper towels in each shell and wrap individually. Store in a rigid container.

Vegetable oil or lard for deep frying corn tortillas

1. Heat 3 or more inches of oil in an electric deep fryer or heavy Dutch oven to 375°F (use a deep-frying or candy thermometer to test).
2. Place tortillas in a taco fryer or use two pairs of tongs to hold the tortilla. Fry one side until slightly crisp but still flexible. Turn the tortilla and with the tongs fold it into a U-shape and hold it in shape in the deep fat using the tongs while completing the frying. Fry about 1½ minutes until crisp and golden; when the bubbles subside, the shells are ready.
3. Drain well on paper towels. Place on taco rack if available or stuff a wad of paper towel in the fold to help the shell retain its shape. Keep warm in a 200°F oven until all are fried.

BEGINNER'S BEEF TACOS

A tasty introduction to the taco. The filling can be frozen for up to 3 months.

Yield: 18 tacos

18 taco shells, warmed in a 225°F oven
1½ pounds ground beef
2 cloves garlic, minced
2 teaspoons flour
2 tablespoons mild pure ground red chile
1½ teaspoons hot pure ground red chile
¼ cup water
1 beef bouillon cube
¾ teaspoon salt
2 tablespoons wine vinegar
⅛ teaspoon ground comino
¼ teaspoon ground Mexican oregano
Chopped onion
Shredded lettuce
Grated Monterey Jack or Cheddar cheese (or a 50/50
    combination)
Chopped tomato
Salsa, your choice (pages 49 to 61)

1. Place taco shells in oven to warm. Heat a heavy skillet and brown the meat with the garlic. Stir in the flour and the mild, hot ground chile.

2. Dissolve the bouillon cube in the water and add to beef; add salt, vinegar, comino, and oregano. Simmer, uncovered, for about 10 minutes.

3. Remove shells from the oven and increase temperature to 450°F. Spoon meat filling into taco shells and add chopped onion, lettuce, cheese, and tomato. Then warm briefly for 2 to 3 minutes to melt the cheese. Serve with a side dish of salsa.

EASY BEEF TACOS

By using the Red Taco Base, you can have a meal on the table, start to finish, in 15 minutes for four, twelve, or however many are coming to dinner! The filling can be frozen for up to 1 year. A real convenience for entertaining and a must for family dinners.

Yield: 12 tacos

12 taco shells, warmed in a 225°F oven (see Deep-Fried Taco
    Shells, page 84)
1 pound lean ground beef
½ medium-size onion, finely chopped
1½ tablespoons rolled oats
¼ cup Red Taco Base (see following recipe)
1 medium-size onion, chopped
2 cups finely shredded lettuce
2 cups shredded Monterey Jack/Cheddar cheese combination
1 medium-size ripe tomato, chopped
Any salsa (see pages 49 to 61)

1. Place taco shells in oven to warm. Brown and cook the beef and onion in a skillet; stir in the salt and rolled oats. Add the ¼ cup Red Taco Base and heat thoroughly.

2. Remove warmed taco shells from the oven and increase temperature to 450°F. Assemble the tacos by spooning some meat filling in each shell; then layer with onion, lettuce, grated cheese, and tomato.

3. Return tacos to oven for 2 to 3 minutes to melt the cheese. Serve immediately with a side dish of salsa for topping.

RED TACO BASE

Make a batch of this base and keep it in the refrigerator for up to a month, or freeze it in 1/2-cup containers for up to a year. Simply add 1/2 cup of Red Taco Base to a pound of browned ground beef for enough filling for 12 tacos.

Yield: 3 cups

2 tablespoons lard
2 tablespoons flour
1/4 cup pure ground hot chile
1 cup pure ground mild chile
9 bouillon cubes, dissolved in 1/2 cup hot water
Salt to taste, depending on whether or not bouillon cubes are
    salted
1 cup red wine vinegar
10 cloves garlic, minced
1 teaspoon ground comino (cumin)
1 teaspoon ground oregano

1. Heat the lard in a saucepan over medium heat; stir in the flour and mix well. Stir in all the ground chile and add the bouillon, a little at a time, stirring constantly until smooth.

2. Add the remaining ingredients, return pan to the heat, and simmer gently for 20 minutes, stirring frequently.

PICADILLO TACOS

Spicy, yet sweetened by the fruit in the mixture, this minced meat taco is complemented by wedges of fresh melon or pineapple. This is one of three picadillo recipes in this book—a less spicy version is included in the beef section. You can freeze any leftovers for up to 2 months.

Yield: 12 tacos

1 pound lean beef, coarsely chopped into ½-inch cubes
1 large onion, chopped
1 clove garlic, minced
¼ cup raisins
1 apple, peeled, cored, and chopped
1 large ripe tomato, peeled and chopped
1 jalapeño chile, very finely minced
⅛ teaspoon cloves
½ teaspoon cinnamon
Salt and freshly ground black pepper
12 taco shells, warmed in a 225°F. oven for 5 to 10 minutes
½ cup slivered toasted almonds
2 cups finely shredded lettuce

1. Brown the meat in a heavy skillet; add the onion and garlic and cook for 5 minutes.
2. Add the raisins, apple, tomato, chile, cloves, and cinnamon. Simmer uncovered for about 20 minutes or until meat is tender and fruit is soft. Season to taste with salt and pepper. Meanwhile, warm the taco shells.
3. Spoon about 3 or 4 tablespoons picadillo into warmed taco shells and top with a sprinkle of toasted almonds and some shredded lettuce. Serve immediately.

NOTE: Picadillo is also excellent served over a bed of rice with warmed, soft tortillas on the side. (See pages 127, 160 for other picadillo variations.) For variety, use pineapple, bananas, and pears in the picadillo instead of apples and raisins, but take care not to let these soft fruits cook too much—heat only until fruit is warm.

SHREDDED CHICKEN TACOS

A wonderful snack or light luncheon dish. For convenience, prepare plenty of shredded chicken at one time and freeze for future use in assorted-size packages. It will keep for up to a year.

Yield: 4 to 6 servings

1 pound fresh chicken pieces
Water
½ teaspoon salt
1 teaspoon juice from marinated jalapeño chiles
8 to 12 taco shells
1 clove garlic, crushed
2 cups finely shredded lettuce
1½ cups grated Monterey Jack cheese
1 large tomato, cut in thin wedges
1 medium-size avocado, cut in thin slices
Salsa Verde (see page 56)

1. Place chicken pieces in a pan, add water to barely cover meat, and season with salt and jalapeño juice. Bring to a boil, reduce heat, cover, and simmer for 15 minutes.

2. Turn off heat and let chicken cool completely in the broth. Drain, remove meat from the bones, and shred, using two forks to do so.

3. Place taco shells in a 225°F oven to warm. Thoroughly toss crushed garlic clove with the lettuce.

4. Remove taco shells from oven and increase temperature to 450°F. Assemble tacos by placing into each shell some shredded chicken, lettuce, and cheese. Return them to the oven for 3 or 4 minutes until cheese melts.

5. Garnish with tomato wedges and avocado slices and serve immediately with a side dish of Salsa Verde (page 56).

SPICED CHICKEN TACO

The chicken bits are crunchy and spicy and make a deliciously different taco with a very special salsa. The coated chicken pieces freeze well for up to 3 months.

Yield: 4 servings

¼ cup cornmeal
1½ teaspoons hot pure ground chile
¼ teaspoon ground Mexican oregano
½ teaspoon ground comino
1 teaspoon minced parsley
1 large clove garlic, minced
½ teaspoon salt

½ cup milk
¼ cup flour
½ teaspoon salt
1½ pounds chicken breasts, boned and cut into ¾-inch wide
    strips
8 taco shells
1½ cups shredded lettuce
Creamy Salsa (page 59)

1. Combine first seven ingredients in a shallow dish. Next, combine flour and salt in another shallow dish.
2. Dip chicken pieces in milk, then in flour-salt mixture to coat, then back in milk. Finally, roll chicken in cornmeal mixture.
3. Heat 2 to 3 inches of oil to 350°F and fry the chicken pieces about 2 to 3 minutes or until golden. Drain on paper towelling.
4. Heat the taco shells in a 225°F oven for about 5 minutes; place some shredded lettuce in each shell, top with 3 or 4 pieces of warm chicken and spoon Creamy Salsa over. Serve immediately.

SHREDDED PORK TACOS

Pork is a favorite meat of Southwestern and Mexican cooks and makes a fabulous taco. Make plenty extra for other uses and freeze for up to 3 months. The use of shredded meat is more Old Mexican than New Mexican.

Yield: 12 tacos

12 taco shells
2 tablespoons bacon drippings or lard
3 cups shredded cooked pork
1 medium-size onion, sliced and separated into rings
1 clove garlic, minced
Salt and pepper
1½ cups shredded lettuce
1½ cups grated Monterey Jack cheese
1 large tomato, chopped
Any salsa (pages 49 to 61)

1. Place taco shells in a 225°F oven to warm. Melt the drippings or lard in a skillet. Add the pork and fry over medium high heat until lightly browned. Add onion, garlic, and salt and pepper to taste and cook until onion is soft. Remove shells from oven and increase temperature to 450°F.

2. Place about 4 tablespoons of meat filling in each taco shell; then add the rest of the ingredients in layers.

3. Return assembled tacos to the oven for about 2 to 3 minutes or until cheese melts. Serve immediately with a side dish of salsa.

NOTE: Fresh raw pork can also be used. Brown well, add onion, garlic, salt, and pepper, cover and simmer for 20 minutes or until thoroughly cooked.

SPICY PORK-FILLED SOFT TACOS

Delicioso! Don't freeze the filled taco shells. Puerco de Mole can be frozen for up to 6 months.

Yield: 8 to 12 tacos

1 recipe Puerco de Mole (pages 65–66)
8 to 12 wheat tortillas (eight 10-inch or 12-inch tortillas, or twelve 8-inch tortillas)
2 or 3 jalapeño chiles sliced very thinly
3 cups shredded lettuce
2 large ripe tomatoes, cut in wedges
1 avocado, peeled and sliced into thin wedges, or 1 recipe Guacamole (page 26)
1 pint sour cream, optional

1. Heat the Puerco de Mole in a skillet or saucepan. Warm the tortillas by wrapping them in foil and heating in a 350°F oven for 15 minutes.

2. Spoon Puerco de Mole down the center of each tortilla, put a few jalapeño slices on each, roll up, and serve on plates garnished with a bed of shredded lettuce, tomato wedges, and avocado slices or guacamole. Spoon a dollop of sour cream on top, if desired.

POACHED FISH TACOS

Delicately spiced fish served with a wonderful creamy green salsa.

Yield: 12 tacos

2 cups chicken broth
¼ teaspoon salt
1½ teaspoons lime juice
1 tablespoon juice from a jar of pickled jalapeño chiles
1 pound fish filets from any firm white fish such as cod,
    haddock, or whiting
12 taco shells, warmed
2 cups finely shredded lettuce
6 scallions, very thinly sliced, tops included
1 tomato, sliced in half and then in thin slices
1½ cups grated Monterey Jack cheese
1 recipe Creamy Salsa (page 59)

1. Place broth, salt, lime juice, and jalapeño juice in a skillet. Heat to simmer, add fish filets, and poach until fish turns white, about 5 minutes. Do not overcook. Meanwhile, warm taco shells in a 225°F oven.

2. Remove fish from pan, drain well, and place in a shallow bowl. Flake the fish by gently pulling it apart with two forks.

3. Assemble the tacos by first placing a little lettuce in each warm taco shell. Next, add fish, scallions, grated cheese, and tomato. Stand upright in a baking dish and warm briefly in a preheated 425°F oven until cheese melts, about 2 to 3 minutes.

4. Serve immediately with Creamy Salsa.

CARNE ASADA SOFT TACOS

Summertime grilling with a southwestern flair. These tacos are also excellent with grilled chicken. Great for buffets! Any leftover beef can be frozen for up to 3 months. Do not freeze filled tacos.

Yield: 6 servings

1½ pounds beef filet
12 tortillas, corn or wheat
2 fresh ripe tomatoes, halved and thinly sliced
1 medium-size onion, finely chopped
2 cups shredded lettuce
Red or green salsa (pages 52, 55)
Guacamole (page 26)
1½ cups sour cream

1. Grill the filet and while it is cooking wrap the tortillas in foil and warm them either on the grill or in a 350°F oven for 15 minutes.

2. Place the tomato, onion, and lettuce in serving bowls. Slice the beef thinly and arrange it in a shallow serving bowl. Place the warm tortillas in a napkin-lined basket.

3. Assemble the tacos by first placing a layer of meat on top of the tortillas: then add the tomatoes, onion, lettuce, and salsa. Serve with guacamole and sour cream on the side.

SOFT CHICKEN ENVUELTOS

Mild and easy to make, these are an interesting variation on predictable crisply fried tacos! Leftover chicken can be frozen for up to 1 year; do not freeze filled envueltos.

Yield: 4 or 8 servings

8 corn tortillas
1½ cups shredded cooked chicken (see Shredded Chicken Tacos, page 89)
1 teaspoon fresh minced cilantro
Salt
1 small clove garlic, crushed
4 green chiles, parched and peeled (page 13), chopped
¾ cup sour cream
1 teaspoon jalapeño chile juice, or to taste
1½ cups shredded lettuce
8 cherry tomatoes
1 large ripe avocado, peeled, pitted, and sliced in wedges

1. Wrap the tortillas in foil and warm them in a 300°F oven along with serving plates.

2. Mix hot, freshly cooked chicken with cilantro, salt, garlic, and chopped chiles.

3. Spoon chicken mixture down the center of each tortilla, roll, and place seam side down on serving plates. Place in oven until warmed through.

4. Mix the sour cream and jalapeño juice. Serve the envueltos topped with sour cream and garnished with shredded lettuce, cherry tomatoes, and avocado wedges.

THE "TACO BAR"

Easy for the hostess and fun for the guests, the "taco bar" lends itself to casual entertaining. It's a terrific idea for an al fresco fiesta, a kid's party, or a pool-side feast.

Preparation of all meats and condiments for the taco bar can be done well in advance, and makes a colorful eye-catching display on a buffet table. Diners assemble their own tacos; no two tacos will be alike!

Prepare bowls of an assortment of the following:

> Fresh tomatoes, chopped
> Fresh serrano chiles, sliced in thin strips
> Pickled jalapeño chiles, thinly sliced
> Radishes, sliced
> Green pepper, chopped
> Spanish onions, sliced very thin and separated into rings
> Scallions, thinly sliced, tops included
> Fresh cilantro, minced
> Chives, snipped
> Monterey Jack cheese, coarsely shredded
> Cheddar cheese, coarsely shredded
> Sour cream
> Pitted black olives, sliced
> Assorted salsas—mild and picante, red and green (2 or 3
>   types)

At serving time, set out baskets of:

> Crisp taco shells
> Warm corn tortillas
> Warm wheat tortillas

Have two or three types of meat fillings in chafing dishes or warmed and brought to the table, such as:

> Bowl of red chile
> Shredded chicken

Pork taco filling
Crumbled and fried chorizo sausage
Shrimp in Nut Sauce (pages 168–69)
Cooked crabmeat
Picadillo (page 160)

And a big bowl of piping hot Frijoles Refritos (page 183) and some Guacamole (page 26) are added bonuses, either to put on the taco or to serve on the side!

CARNE ADOBADA SOFT TACOS

What a way to use leftovers! Carne Adobada freezes well for up to 3 months.

Yield: 12 tacos

12 wheat tortillas
3 cups, approximately, Carne Adobada (see page 163)
1 onion, thinly sliced and separated into rings
2 cups shredded lettuce
1 large ripe tomato, thinly sliced
2 cups grated Cheddar or Monterey Jack cheese, or in combination
Guacamole (see page 26) or sliced avocado

1. Wrap tortillas in foil and place in a 350°F oven to warm. Heat the Carne Adobada.
2. Remove tortillas from oven and increase oven temperature to 425°F. Assemble the tacos by placing some of the warmed meat and sauce along the center of each warm tortilla; then top with some onion, lettuce, sliced tomato, and cheese. Roll up and place on an oven-proof platter.
3. Return tacos to the oven for 5 minutes to melt the cheese. Serve with a garnish of guacamole or avocado slices.

Tostados

A meal on an edible plate, tostados lend themselves wonderfully to buffet entertaining. Put the mixtures in bowls and let your guests make their own dinners.

The tortillas for tostados are always fried crisp and are usually left flat simply by frying on both sides in about 1 inch of lard or oil, but you may want to use the directions included here to form them into the fancy shapes being popularized by restaurants.

BEEF TOSTADOS

The original! The sauce can be frozen for up to 3 months.

Chilied Beef Sauce (recipe follows)
3 cups Frijoles Refritos (page 183)
1 jalapeño chile, chopped, or to taste
1 medium-size Spanish onion, thinly sliced
8 corn tortillas, fried crisp and left flat
9 ounces sharp Cheddar cheese, cut into thin strips
Salad Mixture (recipe follows)
1 avocado, peeled and sliced into thin strips
1 cup shredded Monterey Jack cheese
Salsa Colorado (page 54)

1. Make the Chilied Beef Sauce and keep it warm. Heat the beans with the jalapeño and onion.

2. Place a crisp-fried tortilla on each of six oven-proof serving plates. Spread each with bean mixture and top with strips of Cheddar cheese. Preheat the oven to 325°F.

3. Next, top with the beef sauce and heat for 25 to 30 minutes.

4. To serve, top each with Salad Mixture, and garnish with the avocado strips and shredded Monterey Jack cheese. Serve Salsa Colorado on the side.

Chilied Beef Sauce

1¼ pounds stewing beef, cut into ½-inch cubes
1 tablespoon lard
1 medium-size onion, chopped
2 cloves garlic, minced
1¼ cups Red Chile Sauce (page 52)
Salt to taste

1. Brown the beef in the fat in a heavy skillet over medium heat. Add the onion and garlic and cook until onion is soft.

2. Add the Red Chile Sauce and salt to taste. Simmer for 1 to 2 hours until meat is very tender and flavors blend.

Salad Mixture

3 scallions, thinly sliced
½ cup sliced pitted ripe olives
1 ripe tomato, cut in thin wedges
2½ cups finely shredded lettuce
Salt to taste
8 thin slices purple Bermuda onion, optional

1. Just before serving, combine all ingredients except onion slices, and spoon on top of the meat sauce. Top with onion slices.

MIXED SEAFOOD TOSTADOS

A delightful salad for luncheon or light supper.

Yield: 6 to 8 servings

1½ cups water
½ pound fresh shrimp
2 cups chicken stock
¼ teaspoon salt
1 tablespoon juice from pickled jalapeño chiles
1½ teaspoons fresh lime juice
½ pound bay scallops (or quartered sea scallops)
½ pound cod, flounder, or other firm-fleshed white fish, cut
   in 1½ inch pieces
12 wheat Shaped Tostado Shells (page 22)
3 cups shredded lettuce
Guacamole (page 26)
Salsa Fresca (page 50)

1. Bring 1½ cups water to a boil, add shrimp, and cook until
pink, about 2 minutes. Drain and set aside.
2. At the same time, bring chicken stock, salt, jalapeño juice,
and lime juice to a boil. Add scallops and fish, cover, and poach
over low heat until fish is opaque, about 7 minutes. Do not
overcook. Drain and set aside.
3. Place shredded lettuce in Tostado Shells, then add shrimp,
fish, and scallops. Spoon Guacamole over each and top with
Salsa Fresca.

SHAPED TOSTADO SHELLS

Packed carefully and sealed airtight, these shells can be frozen for up to 1 year.

> 1 empty can (10-ounce size for 6-inch tortillas—use larger can for larger tortillas)
> Corn or wheat tortillas, any size
> 2 quarts cooking oil

1. With a pointed can opener, puncture the can in four places along the bottom *sides* of the can. Then stagger four more punctures on the flat bottom of the can.

2. Heat oil in a deep fryer or 5-quart saucepan to 375°F. Fry shells by floating a tortilla, first-baked side up, and *immediately* centering the punctured can on top.

3. Using two pairs of tongs, press the can into the oil so the tortilla folds up around it as it fries. Leave the can and tortilla submerged for no more than 20 to 25 seconds—you will feel the tortilla harden around the can.

4. Lift can from the oil, pouring off excess oil, and gently lift off the tostado shell. Drain on paper towelling.

NOTES: Commercial tostado fryers are now available in many housewares and department stores. When using shaped shells for tostados, you may want to serve two per person, since they don't hold as much as a flat tostado. These shells fry beautifully when using either corn or wheat tortillas.

CRABMEAT COMPUESTA

Old San Diego (Old Town), the site of California's first mission (established in 1769 by Father Junipero Serra), boasts of many fascinating historic sites and many wonderful restaurants serving such ocean delights as this.

Yield: 6 servings

3 cups refried beans
6 crisp-fried tortillas, corn or wheat, warmed in a 225°F oven
2 avocados
1 scallion, sliced thin
1 clove garlic, mashed
1 teaspoon finely chopped jalapeño chile
1½ tablespoons fresh lime juice (add a little at a time, to taste)
4 to 5 cups finely shredded lettuce
1½ cups shredded Longhorn or mild Cheddar cheese
1 to 1¼ pounds cooked crabmeat
¾ cup pitted ripe olives, halved
12 cherry tomatoes
Salsa Verde (page 56)

1. Heat beans in a saucepan: keep warm. Warm the tostados.

2. Peel and pit the avocado. In a medium-size bowl, mash the avocado, and then mix in the scallion, garlic, jalapeño chile, and lime juice to taste.

3. Divide the lettuce evenly on 6 plates; top with a crisp-fried tortilla. Place hot beans on top and sprinkle with cheese and the crabmeat.

4. Top with avocado mixture, sprinkle with a bit more cheese, and garnish with olive halves and cherry tomatoes.

5. Serve immediately while beans are still hot with Salsa Verde.

Burritos

Easy to make and tremendously versatile, the burrito has increased in popularity with the recent popularity of fast food Mexican shops. Burritos are made with soft wheat tortillas. They are filled (the originals were filled with refried beans), rolled, topped with cheese, warmed in the oven, and served with a sauce. Start from scratch or use leftovers—meat, fish, luncheon meats, vegetables, eggs, and numerous kinds of cheeses can be combined in many different ways to make a tasty lunch or a quick and delicious supper. Use fresh homemade wheat tortillas, if possible—they're so easy to make and so, so good!

BURRITO SANTA FE

This traditional burrito may be similar to the one served to Cortez's armies over 400 years ago. A must to serve with any of the warmed red or green chile sauces.

Yield: 4 servings

4 wheat tortillas (12-inch diameter)
1½ cups Frijoles Refritos (page 183)
2 cups, approximately, Shredded Beef (pages 159–60)
⅓ cup sliced pitted black olives
Any warmed red or green chile sauce (pages 52–55)
1½ cups grated Monterey Jack cheese
Shredded lettuce
Guacamole (page 26)

1. Wrap tortillas in foil and warm in 350°F oven for 15 minutes.
2. Spread refritos down the center of each tortilla and top with shredded beef and sliced olives. Roll and place in a baking dish. Spoon a little salsa over, top with the grated cheese, and bake at 350°F until cheese is melted, about 10 minutes.
3. Serve piping hot on plates garnished with shredded lettuce and Guacamole. Serve additional warmed sauce in a separate bowl.

VARIATION: Add cooked pork or chicken, if desired.

HAM AND CHEESE BURRITO

The Deep South's influence is felt here!

Yield: 4 servings

4 wheat 12-inch tortillas
12 ounces boiled, fully cooked sliced ham
1½ cups grated Monterey Jack or Cheddar cheese
½ cup Coleslaw (page 73) or shredded cabbage or lettuce
Salsa Verde (page 56)

1. Wrap the tortillas in foil, place on serving plates, and heat in a 300°F oven for 15 minutes. While tortillas are warming, fry ham slices in a skillet until hot and lightly browned.

2. Assemble burritos by placing the ham, ¾ cup of the cheese, the cole slaw, and a little salsa lengthwise down the center of each tortilla.

3. Roll the filled tortillas and place in a baking dish. Top with the remaining ¾ cup grated cheese and more salsa. Place in oven and bake briefly until cheese is melted. Serve immediately with additional salsa on the side.

CHICKEN BURRITOS

One of my favorites!

Yield: 4 servings

    4 wheat tortillas (12-inch size)
    1 recipe Salsa Verde (page 56)
    1½ cups Refritos (page 183), warmed
    2 cups cooked chicken, in bite-size pieces
    1 avocado, peeled, pitted, and sliced in thin wedges
    2 scallions, chopped, tops included
    2 cups grated Cheddar or Monterey Jack cheese
    1 small or medium-size tomato, chopped
    Lettuce leaves
    ½ cup sour cream

1. Wrap tortillas in foil, place on serving plates, and warm in a 300°F oven for 10 or 15 minutes. Warm sauce in a small saucepan.

2. Spread Refritos down the center of each tortilla; then add chicken, avocado wedges, scallions, 1 cup of the cheese, and chopped tomato. Roll the burritos and place on the plates. Top with the other cup of the cheese.

3. Bake at 350°F for about 10 minutes until cheese melts.

4. Serve immediately on lettuce leaves with sauce spooned over the top of each, then add a dollop of sour cream.

FISH FILET BURRITOS

Neptune's best burrito bet!

Yield: 4 servings

4 wheat 12-inch tortillas
1 pound fish filets (use a firm fish such as cod, ocean perch,
    etc.)
Flour
Salt and freshly ground black pepper
4 to 6 tablespoons butter
2 scallions, finely chopped
1½ cups grated Monterey Jack cheese
2 cups coarsely chopped lettuce
Salsa Ranchero (page 58)

1. Wrap the tortillas in foil and warm them in a 350°F oven for 15 minutes.

2. Sprinkle the fish filets lightly with flour, salt, and pepper. Heat the butter in a heavy skillet and fry the filets until browned and cooked, about 10 minutes.

3. Place the filets down the center of each warm tortilla and sprinkle with a few scallions and a little of the grated cheese (reserve about 1 cup for topping). Roll and place on four plates. Sprinkle tops with remaining cheese.

4. Bake at 300°F for 10 to 15 minutes, until cheese is melted.

5. Nest each with shredded lettuce and serve with Salsa Ranchero (page 58).

SHEEPHERDER'S SANDWICH

A simple sandwich with great versatility.

Yield: 4 servings

4 wheat tortillas (8-inch diameter)
¾ pound (approximately) pastrami
4 or more fresh green chiles (hot or mild), parched and
   peeled (page 13), sliced in long, thin strips
2 tablespoons olive oil
3 tablespoons vinegar
2 tablespoons water

1. Wrap the tortillas in foil. Wrap the pastrami in foil. Heat both in the same oven at 350°F for about 15 minutes.

2. While tortillas and pastrami are warming, place chiles, oil, vinegar, and water in a small saucepan. Bring to a boil, reduce heat, and simmer for 5 minutes.

3. To assemble sandwiches, lay slices of hot pastrami along the center of each warm tortilla about two-thirds of the way down the length. Evenly divide the warmed green chile over the meat. Fold the bottom one-third of the tortilla up, then fold the two sides over the pastrami and chiles. The sandwich will then be closed at one end to prevent dripping.

VARIATIONS: Substitute ham for pastrami; use salami, spicy salsa, and grated cheese; or roast beef, chopped onion, and tomato salsa. The combinations are endless!

Chimichangos and Flautas

Chimichangos are relatively new arrivals to the Tex-Mex cooking scene. These filled wheat tortillas are similar to burritos but differ in that they are folded and deep-fried. For other chimichango variations, use any of the taco or burrito fillings included in this book.

Flautas (Spanish for flute) are lesser known than tacos, yet are very similar. They derive their name from their appearance after being rolled and deep-fried.

TUCSON CHIMICHANGOS

The greatest! And my favorite traditional filling! I developed this filling after several testing and tasting sessions following unsuccessful attempts to get restauranteurs to share their secrets. It can be frozen for up to 3 months.

Yield: 6 servings

2 pounds stewing beef, coarsely chopped
2 medium-size potatoes, diced small
8 large hot green chiles, parched and peeled (page 13), chopped
2 cloves garlic, minced
1 large onion, chopped
1 ½ teaspoons salt
1 teaspoon ground Mexican oregano
¼ teaspoon ground comino (cumin)
Water
12 wheat tortillas
Lard or vegetable oil for deep frying
2 cups shredded lettuce
2 ripe tomatoes, cut into wedges
1 recipe Red Chile Sauce (page 52)
1 pint sour cream

1. In a skillet or saucepan, place the beef, potatoes, chiles, garlic, onion, salt, oregano, and comino. Add just enough water to cover. Simmer, covered, for at least 1 hour, or until well done and very tender. The mixture should be quite thick; if too "soupy," remove lid and cook until some of the liquid has evaporated.

2. Meanwhile, wrap the tortillas in foil and warm them in a 325°F oven for 15 minutes.

3. Divide the filling among the 12 tortillas, placing about 2 heaping tablespoons in the center of each. Fold one side of the

tortilla over the filling, then the two adjacent sides, and finally fold the fourth side over. Secure with a toothpick.

4. Heat about 2 inches of lard to 375°F in a heavy skillet. Fry the filled tortillas until golden, turning to brown evenly. Drain well on paper towelling.

5. Place 2 chimichangos on each of six plates and keep them warm in a 250°F oven.

6. Serve piping hot surrounded on the plate by shredded lettuce and tomato wedges. Spoon Red Chile Sauce on top of each and center with generous dollops of sour cream.

CHORIZO CHIMICHANGOS

Spicy sausage and melted cheese team up to make these delicious chimichangos.

Yield: 6 servings

12 wheat tortillas
Lard or vegetable oil for frying
1½ pounds chorizo sausage (page 188)
2 medium-size tomatoes, chopped
1 medium-size onion, chopped, or 3 to 4 thinly sliced
    scallions with tops
2 cups grated Monterey Jack cheese
2 cups shredded lettuce
Salsa Fresca (page 50)
1 cup sour cream

1. Wrap the tortillas in foil and warm them in a 300°F oven for 15 minutes. In a deep, heavy skillet, preheat about 2 inches of lard or oil to 375°F.

2. While tortillas are warming, crumble and brown sausage in a heavy skillet; cook thoroughly and drain off fat. Stir in the chopped tomatoes.

3. Place equal amounts of the sausage-tomato mixture on each of the 12 tortillas. Sprinkle each with onion and grated cheese.

4. Fold as for Tucson Chimichangos. Fry in 2 inches of hot lard until evenly browned; drain and place on six plates in a 250°F oven to keep warm until all are fried.

5. Serve hot surrounded by shredded lettuce, topped with Salsa Fresca and a dollop of sour cream.

GREEN CHILE AND CHICKEN CHIMICHANGOS

Yield: 6 servings

12 wheat tortillas
Lard or vegetable oil for frying
2 cups cooked chicken, diced
4 to 6 green chiles, parched and peeled (page 13), chopped
¼ teaspoon ground comino (cumin)
Salt and freshly ground black pepper
2 cups grated Monterey Jack cheese
⅔ cup sour cream
Shredded lettuce
Sour cream
Salsa Verde or hot green sauce (see pages 55, 56)

1. Wrap the tortillas in foil and warm them in a 300°F. oven for 15 minutes. Heat 2 inches of lard or oil to 375°F.

2. Combine the chicken, chiles, comino, salt and pepper to taste, cheese, and ⅔ cup sour cream.

3. Place equal amounts of the chicken mixture on each of the tortillas. Fold as for Tucson Chimichangos. Fry in 2 inches of hot lard until evenly browned; drain and keep warm in oven until all are fried.

4. Place 2 chimichangos on each of six warmed plates. Garnish with shredded lettuce and top with a dollop of the additional sour cream and Salsa Verde or hot green sauce.

FLAUTAS

Flautas got their name from their "flute-like" shape. These tacos can be filled with various combinations of ingredients.

Yield: 4 to 6 servings

12 corn tortillas, warmed
2 cups cooked meat filling (see Tacos, pages 83–97)
1 quart lard or cooking oil
2 cups shredded lettuce
2 cups Guacamole (page 26) or sour cream
1 recipe any salsa (pages 49–61)

1. Wrap the tortillas in foil and heat in the oven for about 15 minutes to soften them. In a deep, heavy skillet, heat about 1 inch of lard to 375°F.

2. Place about 2 tablespoons filling in a narrow strip down the center of each tortilla. Roll tightly and secure with toothpicks.

3. Fry flautas in the hot lard; turn to brown evenly. Drain well on paper towelling.

4. Place on a bed of shredded lettuce; garnish with Guacamole or sour cream on top and serve with salsa.

Enchiladas

Enchiladas are a definite favorite on both Mexican and south-western tables. These "chilied" tortillas are extremely versatile. The traditional Mexican enchilada consists of a lightly fried tortilla dipped in Red Chile Sauce (see page 52), which is then filled with cheese and possibly onions, rolled, and baked with more sauce spooned over it. But authentic Rio Grande enchiladas are served stacked open-faced with filling between the layers of tortillas. . . and with a poached or sunny-side up egg on top.

Beans, shredded or ground beef, shredded pork or chicken, eggs, chorizo, seafood or fish, cheese and onions in various combinations all make wonderful fillings; or the meat can be added directly to the sauce and spooned atop the stacked tortillas.

As a party entree, enchiladas are a real plus. They can be prepared one or even two days ahead, placed in a casserole and refrigerated until ready to use. At serving time, just spoon more sauce over and heat through.

The three basic steps in preparing enchiladas are:
1) lightly fry the tortilla in hot oil; 2) dip the fried tortilla in sauce, or spoon sauce over each if making stacked enchiladas; and 3) fill and shape the enchiladas. They can be prepared as individual servings on oven-proof serving plates or placed in a casserole for a crowd. Two or three enchiladas usually make an ample serving. Serve enchiladas garnished with shredded lettuce, tomatoes, and guacamole, if desired.

SANTA FE STYLE ENCHILADAS

The meat mixture and Red Chile Sauce can each be frozen separately for up to 6 months.

Yield: 4 servings

2 tablespoons lard
1 medium-size onion, chopped
1 clove garlic, minced
1 pound ground lean beef or 2 cups cooked shredded beef
½ teaspoon ground comino
2 cups grated Cheddar or Monterey Jack cheese, or in combination
12 corn tortillas
Oil for frying
3 cups Red Chile Sauce (1½ recipes)
1 fresh ripe tomato, cut in 8 wedges
1 chopped fresh onion
4 poached or lightly fried eggs
Coarsely chopped lettuce

1. Heat the lard in a skillet; sauté the onion and garlic until onion is soft. Add the hamburger and comino; simmer for 15 minutes.

2. Meanwhile, lightly fry the tortillas in shallow oil over medium heat (they should remain very soft); then drain on paper towel. Heat four plates in a 350°F oven.

3. Put a little Red Chile Sauce on each plate, top with a tortilla, spoon a little meat mixture on top, and then add a light sprinkling of cheese, onion, and more sauce. Repeat twice more, and top each completed stack with more Red Chile Sauce and cheese.

4. Return plates to oven and heat until cheese melts. Top each with a cooked egg; then surround each tortilla stack with chopped lettuce and 2 wedges of tomato and serve.

RED CHILE ENCHILADAS

Yield: 4 servings

12 corn tortillas
Lard or vegetable oil for frying
3 cups Red Chile Sauce (1½ recipes)
2 cups grated 50/50 mixture of Monterey Jack and sharp
    Cheddar cheese
1 large onion, chopped
1 cup sour cream, optional
2 cups shredded lettuce
2 medium-size tomatoes, cut in wedges

1. Lightly fry the tortillas in about ½ inch of lard or oil. Drain on paper towel. Meanwhile, warm four plates in a 300°F oven.

2. Dip each tortilla in sauce; then place a strip of grated cheese and chopped onion down the center. Roll and place 3 enchiladas on each plate. Top with more sauce and cheese.

3. Bake at 350°F until cheese is melted. Top each serving with a dollop of sour cream, if desired, and garnish the plates with shredded lettuce and tomato wedges.

NOTE: For a party or for entertaining, place enchiladas in a casserole. This can be done a day or two ahead of time and refrigerated. Add sauce and sprinkle with cheese and onion and warm until cheese bubbles, about 10 to 15 minutes.

ENCHILADAS SUISAS

Casserole enchiladas with heavy cream.

Yield: 4 to 6 servings

1 recipe Salsa Verde (page 56)
12 corn tortillas
Vegetable oil for frying
2 cups shredded cooked chicken or pork
1 cup grated Monterey Jack cheese
1 cup grated mild Cheddar cheese
1 cup heavy cream
¼ cup chopped scallions, tops included
Black olives
Cherry tomatoes

1. Prepare Salsa Verde; set aside. In a heavy skillet, lightly fry the tortillas in shallow oil being careful not to make them too crisp to roll. Combine the two cheeses and set ½ cup aside for topping.

2. Dip each tortilla in Salsa Verde (both sides); place 2 heaping tablespoons chicken or pork and about 2 tablespoons cheese down the center of each; roll and place seam side down in a shallow baking dish.

3. After all the rolled tortillas are in the dish, spoon additional Salsa Verde over them, and then cover evenly with 1 cup of heavy cream. Sprinkle with remaining ½ cup cheese and with the scallions, and bake, uncovered, at 350°F for 20 minutes.

4. Serve immediately, garnished with black olives and cherry tomatoes and with additional salsa on the side.

GREEN CHILE ENCHILADAS

Make these and make plenty of them. A delicious and festive meal that everyone is certain to love! The meat sauce can be frozen for up to 3 months.

Yield: 4 servings

3 tablespoons flour
4 cups beef broth
1½ to 2 cups shredded or chopped cooked beef or pork
¾ cup green chiles, parched and peeled (see page 13), chopped, or more to taste
1 teaspoon ground comino
1 clove garlic, minced
Salt
Freshly ground black pepper
12 corn tortillas
Oil for frying
2 cups sour cream
1 medium-size onion, chopped
1¾ cups grated Cheddar or Monterey Jack cheese
Coarsely chopped lettuce
Fresh tomato wedges

1. Mix the flour with ¼ cup of the beef broth to make a smooth paste; then combine with the remaining broth in a medium-size saucepan. Cook until slightly thickened. Add the beef or pork, chiles, comino, garlic, salt, and pepper. Keep mixture warm.
2. In a skillet, lightly fry the tortillas in ½ inch of hot oil. Warm four plates in the oven.
3. Combine sour cream, onion, and 1 cup of the grated cheese.
4. Assemble the enchiladas by placing a spoonful of sauce on each plate, then a tortilla, more sauce, and a spoonful of sour cream mixture. Continue until each plate has 3 tortillas and all the sauce is used. Top each with a generous dollop of sour cream mixture and the remaining grated cheese.

5. Return the plates to the oven and heat at 375°F until cheese melts. Serve garnished with chopped lettuce and tomato wedges.

NOTE: These enchiladas are also excellent when prepared with chicken. When chicken is used, substitute chicken broth for beef broth.

CRABMEAT ENCHILADAS WITH GREEN CHILE

This recipe possibly originated in Old Sacramento—at least that's where I first discovered it!

Yield: 4 servings

> 8 corn tortillas
> Vegetable oil for frying
> 2 cups Salsa Verde (see page 56)
> 2 cups cooked crabmeat, fresh or frozen
> 5 scallions, chopped, tops included
> 1½ cups sour cream
> 1½ cups grated Monterey Jack cheese
> ½ cup sliced green olives
> Lettuce, coarsely chopped

1. In a heavy skillet, lightly fry the tortillas in about ½ inch of oil. Drain on absorbent paper towels. Warm four plates in the oven.
2. Dip each tortilla in Salsa Verde and place 2 on each plate.
3. Place ¼ cup crabmeat along the center of each tortilla, sprinkle with scallions, and add a spoonful of sauce. Roll and place seam side down on plates.
4. Mix sour cream and grated cheese, spoon about ⅓ cup over each tortilla, and sprinkle olive slices on top. Return to oven and heat at 350°F for about 10 to 15 minutes. Serve surrounded by chopped lettuce and with additional Salsa Verde.

CHILE DISHES

Chiles Rellenos

Chiles rellenos are simply stuffed chiles. North of the border, the favorite filling among "gringos" is cheese, with the chiles dipped in a heavy batter; Indian or native families often prefer a picadillo-type filling. And in Old Mexico, the poblano chile, which resembles our sweet bell pepper, is stuffed with goat cheese and dipped in an egg batter.

Chiles rellenos are best when fried just before serving, but the chiles and batter can be prepared separately well in advance. As a matter of fact, I would advise stuffing the chiles several hours before you plan to serve them, and letting them rest between layers of paper towels—the batter will adhere better. If you *must* fry the chiles ahead of time, drain them well and place in a single layer on paper towels. Refry them briefly to heat through and drain again.

Any leftover chiles can be frozen between layers of wax paper and stored in a rigid container. Reheat them under the broiler or cut them into 1-inch slices and serve as an hors d'oeuvre.

If you're serving chiles rellenos as a main course, round out the meal with red or green chile sauce, tossed salad or guacamole, and refritos or posole.

CHILES RELLENOS DE QUESO

The traditional chile relleno. Serve as a main dish or as a vegetable dish.

Yield: 4 to 6 servings

12 large, mild green chiles, parched and peeled (page 13),
   with stems on (If chiles are unavailable, substitute bell or
   Italian frying peppers or three 4-ounce cans of green
   chiles.)
8 ounces Monterey Jack cheese, cut into 12 long, narrow
   strips
1 recipe Batter I or II (page 129)
Vegetable oil or lard for frying

1. Peel the chiles, leaving the stems on. Cut a small slit just below the stem and, if desired, remove the seeds (if using mild peppers, this may not be necessary). Being careful not to split the chiles, insert the strips of cheese. Drain well on paper towels to ensure adhesion of the batter.

2. Prepare your choice of batters.

3. Preheat at least 2 inches of oil to 375°F in a deep heavy skillet, large saucepan, or deep fryer, using a thermometer to reach an accurate temperature. Dip the stuffed chiles in the batter and fry until golden. Two tongs work best to hold and turn them. Drain well on paper towels.

4. Serve piping hot with red or green chile sauce (pages 52, 55).

CHILES RELLENOS PICADILLO

Yield: 4 to 6 servings

2 tablespoons lard or bacon fat
1 pound beef chuck, cut into ½-inch cubes
2 cloves garlic, minced
¼ cup chopped onion
1 cup water
½ teaspoon ground cloves
2 teaspoons ground coriander (cilantro in Spanish)
¾ teaspoon salt
1 cup raisins
12 large, mild green chiles, prepared as for Chiles Rellenos
    de Queso (page 126)
1 recipe Batter II (page 129)

1. Melt the lard and brown the meat in a heavy skillet. Add garlic and onions and sauté until onions are transparent. Add 1 cup water, cover, and simmer until meat is tender, about 1 hour.

2. Add cloves, coriander, salt, and raisins and simmer, uncovered, until meat mixture is thick but still moist. Cool.

3. Stuff the prepared chiles with the meat mixture, coat with batter, and fry until golden in 2 or more inches of oil heated to 375°F. Drain and serve piping hot with or without chile salsa or a tomato salsa.

VARIATION: You can use 12 dried green chiles instead of fresh. Soak them in a little warm water to soften, coarsely chop them, and stir them into the meat mixture. Form the meat mixture into oval shapes. Dip the ovals in flour. Beat 3 egg whites until stiff and use this meringue for coating instead of batter. Deep fry at 375°F until golden.

BAKED CORN-STUFFED CHILES RELLENOS

A simplified way to prepare chiles rellenos. The flavor remains but the chiles are softer in texture.

Yield: 4 to 6 servings

2 tablespoons lard or bacon fat
1 medium-size onion, chopped
1 clove garlic, minced
¼ to ½ teaspoon salt
Freshly ground black pepper
Pinch of ground Mexican oregano
Ranchero Sauce (page 58), optional
3 cups fresh or frozen corn kernels
1 large fresh tomato, peeled and chopped
2½ cups shredded Monterey Jack or mild Cheddar cheese
    (reserve ½ cup for topping)
12 green chiles, prepared as for Chiles Rellenos de Queso
    (page 126)
1 cup light or medium cream

1. Heat fat in a large, heavy skillet. Sauté onion and garlic until onion is soft. Add salt, pepper, oregano, corn, and tomato and simmer, uncovered, for 15 to 20 minutes, to reduce the liquid. Remove from heat. Meanwhile, prepare Ranchero Sauce (page 58).

2. Stir 2 cups of the grated cheese into the corn mixture. Cool.

3. Stuff the chiles with the mixture and place them in a large, shallow baking dish. Evenly pour the cream over the chiles and sprinkle with the reserved ½ cup cheese.

4. Bake at 375°F for 25 minutes or until sauce is bubbly and cheese is lightly browned.

BATTER I—NEW MEXICO-STYLE BATTER

Crisp and crunchy. I like this batter best when made with blue cornmeal.

> 1 cup flour
> 1 teaspoon baking powder
> ½ teaspoon salt
> ¾ cup cornmeal—blue, white, or yellow
> 1 cup milk
> 2 eggs

1. In a medium-size bowl, combine flour, baking powder, salt, and cornmeal.
2. Blend the milk and eggs, then add to the dry ingredients. Mix until smooth. If necessary, add a little more milk to achieve a smooth batter that will adhere to the chiles.

BATTER II—CALIFORNIA-STYLE BATTER

A light, airy, puffed batter.

> 4½ tablespoons flour
> ¾ teaspoon baking powder
> ¼ teaspoon salt
> 4 eggs, separated

1. Thoroughly combine the dry ingredients.
2. Beat egg whites until stiff but not dry. In a medium-size bowl, beat egg yolks until thick; add the dry ingredients and blend well.
3. Gently fold in the egg whites.

Chile con Carne

Very often thought of as Mexican, chili con carne as we know it is an authentic American creation . . . and full of controversy about its beginnings. In the Southwest, beans are not put in chili; instead, they are served on the side.

All the recipes included here freeze very well, so make big batches for convenience, it's much easier to make a triple batch than to make three single recipes!

Incidentally, leftover chili con carne is great piled into crisp taco shells or soft warm wheat tortillas. It's also a delicious addition to omelets and souffles. Pour over hamburgers and hot dogs for a nice treat, or use as the basis for tamale pie. The list is endless!

PECOS VALLEY BOWL OF RED

My personal favorite, Bowl of Red was adapted from the first Texas chili cook-off winner's recipe. A true Dallas-type chili, it contains no beans and no tomatoes, just hearty beef and chile. Great served with side dishes of mixin's and fixin's. For fixin's, I serve chopped Spanish onions, jalapeño slices, sour cream with fresh lime, and a coarsely grated 50/50 mixture of Monterey Jack and full cream sharp Cheddar. The Bowl of Red can be frozen for up to a year.

Yield: 8 to 10 servings

1 tablespoon lard, bacon drippings, or butter
1 large Spanish onion, coarsely chopped
3 pounds lean beef, such as chuck, cut in ½-to 1-inch cubes
    or coarsely chopped or ground. (Have the butcher use his
    ½-inch plate—the same one used for making Italian
    sausage)
3 cloves garlic, chopped
4 tablespoons ground pure mild red chile
4 tablespoons ground pure hot red chile
1 tablespoon ground comino (cumin)
3 cups water
2 teaspoons salt

1. Melt the fat in a heavy Dutch oven and sauté the onion.
2. Mix the meat with the garlic, chiles, and comino. Add the meat and seasonings to the pot, cook for 15 minutes or until the pink color disappears.
3. Add the remaining ingredients; stir well. Simmer 3 or 4 more hours until the meat is very tender and the flavors are well blended. Add additional water as needed. Taste and add more seasonings, if desired.

CARNE COLORADO

Straight from the Rio Grande—the New Mexican version of what Texans labeled chile con carne. Serve with a side dish of stewed pinto beans, a mixed lettuce salad or coleslaw, and fresh, warm sopaipillas to collect the sauce. This dish can be frozen for up to 6 months.

Yield: 6 to 8 servings

2 tablespoons lard or bacon drippings
2 pounds beef chuck, cut in ½-inch to 1-inch cubes
1 large onion, chopped
2 cloves garlic, minced
½ teaspoon ground comino
½ teaspoon ground Mexican oregano
¼ cup pure ground mild red chile
¼ cup pure ground hot red chile
3 to 4 cups beef broth
1½ teaspoons salt
4 to 6 cups stewed pinto beans

1. Heat the lard in a large, heavy skillet; add the beef cubes and brown well. Stir in the onion and garlic and cook until onion begins to soften.

2. Remove from heat and add the comino, oregano, and ground chile; mix well. Add 3 cups of beef broth. Bring to a boil, reduce heat, and simmer for about 1 hour or until tender, adding more broth as necessary.

3. To serve, ladle beans into bowls; then top with Carne Colorado.

"DEVIL'S BREW"

A real winner! It will freeze well for up to a year.

Yield: 6 to 8 servings

2 tablespoons bacon fat or lard
3 pounds lean beef chuck, cut in ½-inch cubes
½ teaspoon freshly ground black pepper
6 tablespoons pure ground hot chile
3 tablespoons ground comino (cumin)
3 cloves garlic, finely chopped
2 onions, coarsely chopped
Water
¼ cup chile caribe (see page 53)
1 teaspoon dried oregano soaked in ¼ cup warm beer
2 tablespoons pure ground mild chile
1 tablespoon cider vinegar
1½ cups beef broth
3 mild or hot green chiles, chopped (or one 4-ounce can
    diced green chiles, drained)
1 large ripe tomato, chopped
1 tablespoon masa harina (corn flour)

1. Melt fat in a large, heavy pot and brown the meat.

2. Stir in the black pepper, ground chile, comino, garlic, and onions. Add water to barely cover the meat. Bring to a boil; then lower the heat and simmer, uncovered, for 30 to 45 minutes, adding more water as necessary.

3. Stir in the crushed red chiles, the oregano-beer mixture, vinegar, 1 cup of the beef broth, the chopped chiles, and tomato. Simmer, uncovered, for 30 minutes longer, stirring often.

4. Dissolve the masa flour in the remaining ½ cup of beef broth. Stir it into the pot and simmer for another 15 to 20 minutes.

CHESAPEAKE BAY CHILE

A hearty, eastern, and slightly more sophisticated version of chile. You can freeze it for about 4 months.

Yield: 6 to 8 servings

1 tablespoon bacon drippings
1 large onion, chopped
3 pounds lean beef, coarsely chopped or coarsely ground
4 tablespoons pure ground mild chile
2 to 4 tablespoons pure ground hot chile
2 tablespoons ground comino (cumin)
3 cloves garlic, chopped
1 tablespoon Worcestershire sauce
2 teaspoons salt
2 cups water
1 can (8 ounces) tomato sauce
1 can (16 ounces) pinto beans, undrained
Chile Pequín to taste, if desired

1. Melt bacon drippings in a large, heavy pot and brown onion and beef. Add the ground chiles, comino, garlic, and Worcestershire sauce and cook for about 2 minutes.

2. Add salt, tomatoes, and water and cook for about 45 minutes. Add beans and cook for another 10 minutes or longer. Add chile pequín to taste if a hotter flavor is desired.

KANSAS CITY CHILI

Mild-mannered, yet robust—particularly crowd pleasing to novices at chili sampling! It can be frozen for up to 4 months.

Yield: 10 to 12 servings

3 pounds lean beef chuck, coarsely chopped
2 pounds lean hamburger
2 large onions, diced
5 cloves garlic, minced
4 tablespoons pure ground mild chile
2 or 3 tablespoons pure ground hot chile (or more)
1½ tablespoons ground comino (cumin)
1½ tablespoons salt
2 cans (28 ounces each) peeled whole tomatoes
2 cans (15 ounces each) tomato sauce
3 cups water
2 cans (16 ounces each) drained pinto beans, optional

1. In a large, heavy pot or Dutch oven, brown the meat, onions, and garlic, stirring frequently.
2. Add ground chiles and comino. Add salt, tomatoes (break them up with a fork), tomato sauce, and water. Mix thoroughly. Simmer, covered, for about 2 hours or until meat is very tender. Taste and adjust seasonings.
3. If adding beans, add to chili about 30 minutes before serving.

FREEZING TIP: Freezes well for up to 4 months.

Tamales

Tamales (the word means "patties" in the Aztec language) have their roots very firmly embedded in ancient Indian culture. They have been prepared for many, many centuries in kitchens from as far north as Santa Fe, New Mexico, all the way to South America.

Tamales are prepared by spreading a masa (dried ground corn) mixture and a saucy filling on dried corn husks, wrapping and tying the corn husks around the filling, and steaming them. In Oaxaca, Mexico, they substitute banana leaves for corn husks. They're fun to make, especially when done with lots of helping hands.

Tamales freeze very well and can be stored for up to a year. And any leftover masa mixture and fillings can also be frozen separately for later use.

Extremely adaptable, tamales are a great way to salvage leftovers. Fillings and sauces can be red or green. Cooked sauces are usually served over tamales but fresh salsas can also be served. Meats simmered in Mole Sauce (page 61) make delicious tamales with the flavor of Old Mexico from Oaxaca. You can also use the meat fillings, thinned slightly, as sauces for serving over the tamales.

NATIVE NEW MEXICAN TAMALES

There are three basic steps to making these tamales: 1) the filling, 2) the masa, and 3) stuffing and wrapping in softened corn husks. You can package completed tamales in airtight plastic bags in serving-size quantities, and freeze for up to 1 year. When steaming tamales from a frozen state, increase the cooking time by half. Any leftover masa mixture or filling can be stored in sealed containers, labeled, and frozen for later use.

The Filling
Meat Filling in Red Chile Sauce

Yield: enough to make 5 to 6 dozen tamales

1½ pounds meat (pork, stewing beef, chuck, or chicken)
1½ tablespoons bacon drippings
1 clove garlic, minced
½ cup ground pure red chile
¾ teaspoon salt
¼ teaspoon ground Mexican oregano
1 to 2 cups reserved meat stock

1. Simmer the meat in just enough water to cover and cook until tender. Reserve stock.

2. Cut the meat in very small cubes or chop in a food processor. In a heavy skillet, brown the meat in the bacon drippings.

3. After the meat has browned, add the garlic and cook for about 2 minutes. Remove pan from heat, cool slightly, and add the ground chile. Season with salt and oregano.

4. Add a cup of meat stock and simmer the sauce, uncovered, stirring regularly, for 30 to 40 minutes. Continue to add stock little by little as it blends in to make a thick, smooth sauce.

The Masa
Cornmeal Mixture

Yield: enough to make 5 to 6 dozen tamales

3½ cups warm water
6 cups masa (yellow, white, or blue)
2 cups lard
1¾ teaspoons salt

1. Add the 3½ cups warm water to the masa to make a very thick mixture that holds together; then let it stand.

2. Using medium speed on an electric mixer, cream the lard with the salt until very fluffy. Combine the lard with the masa and mix well with the electric mixer.

The Cornhusks
Soaking, Filling, Wrapping, and Steaming

5 to 6 dozen corn husks
Hot water

1. Soak the corn husks in hot water until soft and pliable.

2. Spread about 2 tablespoons of masa mixture on each softened corn husk, making a rectangle about 3 by 4 inches and leaving at least a 2-inch margin of husk around the edges. Next, top the center of the masa with a strip of the meat filling.

3. Fold one side of the husk toward the center, covering the meat filling with the masa; then roll the husk (still lengthwise) to form a long, round tamale. Fold the bottom of the husk up and tie both ends with strips of corn husk, or, fold bottom up and top down and tie together in the center. If you plan to freeze the tamales, do so at this point, before steaming them.

4. Stand the tamales upright on a rack in a large kettle or a pressure cooker. Before the rack is completely filled, add water ¾-inch deep in the bottom of the pot. Steam the tamales in a conventional steamer for 45 minutes, or in a pressure cooker under 15 pounds pressure for 20 minutes.

5. Serve with sauce, either the thinned meat filling in this recipe or the Red Chile Sauce (page 52).

GREEN CHILE AND CHEESE TAMALES

For a pleasant change, serve these instead of tortillas or bread. They can be frozen, before steaming, for up to 1 year.

Yield: 24 tamales

24 corn husks
½ recipe Tamale Masa (pages 138–39)
12 ounces Monterey Jack cheese, cut in 24 strips
8 green chiles (approximately), parched and peeled (page 13),
    cut in strips
¾ cup finely chopped onion

1. Soak the corn husks in hot water until soft and pliable. Spread about 2 tablespoons masa on each corn husk, leaving about a 2-inch margin on all sides. Top with a piece of cheese, strips of chile, and a sprinkling of onion.

2. Roll, tie, and steam according to procedure used in Native New Mexican Tamales (pages 138–39).

3. Serve plain as a "bread" or with red or green chile sauce or Salsa Fresca.

TUCSON TAMALES

This recipe is very different from traditional tamale recipes. When fresh corn is in season, these tamales are a delicious change from red chile tamales. Make many, freeze them, and enjoy them all year long. They will keep frozen in a sealed container for up to a year.

Yield: 24 tamales, approximately

12 ears of fresh yellow or white corn
1 pound Monterey Jack cheese, grated
½ pound butter
1 pound pure lard
⅓ cup (scant) sugar
¼ cup light cream, or more
Salt
24 green chiles, parched and peeled (page 13)
1 pound mild Cheddar cheese, grated
1 recipe Green Chile Sauce (page 55)

1. Cut stalk end of each ear of corn flush with the base of the ear. Shuck corn; be careful to keep corn husks intact for wrapping tamales. Wash and drain husks.

2. Cut corn off cobs. In a food processor or with a meat grinder, grind corn with the Monterey Jack cheese.

3. Using an electric mixer, cream butter and lard until fluffy; add the sugar, cream, salt, and the corn-cheese mixture. Continue beating until the mixture is *very* fluffy, like whipped cream. If mixture seems dry, add a bit more cream.

4. Cut the parched chiles in long strips.

5. Spread about 2 tablespoons of the corn mixture on each husk, leaving at least a 2-inch margin of husk on all sides. Top with about 2 strips of chile; then sprinkle with a little Cheddar cheese.

6. Roll, tie, and steam according to procedure used in Tamale recipe (pages 138–39). If you are planning to freeze the tamales, do so before steaming. Serve warm with Green Chile Sauce (page 55).

BLUE CORN TAMALES—FILLED WITH CHICKEN, CHILES, AND SOUR CREAM

Tamales with a Rio Grande influence. Blue corn is grown by the Pueblo Indians in limited areas along the Rio Grande in New Mexico—Santo Domingo, San Fidel, Isleta, and Santa Clara. Packaged and stored in sealed containers, tamales can be frozen for up to 1 year.

1 chicken—cooked, boned, and shredded (see page 13), about 2 pounds of meat
1 to 2 tablespoons chopped jalapēno chile (depending on taste)
½ cup chopped mild green chile (or, if unavailable, add more finely chopped jalapēno chile)
1 cup sour cream
1 cup grated Monterey Jack cheese
Salt and pepper to taste
½ recipe Blue Corn Masa (see Masa recipe, pages 138–39, and use blue corn masa)
24 corn husks, approximately
1 recipe Green Chile Sauce (page 55)

1. Mix chicken, chiles, sour cream, and cheese. Season with salt and pepper to taste.

2. Prepare the blue corn masa according to directions for Masa (pages 138–39). Meanwhile, soak the corn husks in warm water until softened and pliable.

3. Spread about 2 tablespoons masa mixture on corn husks, leaving about a 2-inch margin on all sides. Place a strip of chicken mixture down the center of the masa. Roll, tie, and steam according to procedure used in Tamale recipe (pages 138–39). Freeze at this point, before steaming, if desired.

4. Heat the Green Chile Sauce and serve over the tamales.

Huevos (Eggs)

Eggs—complemented with the chiles and seasonings of the Southwest—are a wonderful food to serve for breakfast, brunch, or for a simple supper. Tomatoes, chiles, cheese, chorizo, spicy meats, potatoes, and tortillas are delicious in combination with the egg's delicate flavor.

Eggs are very popular in Mexican and Southwestern cooking, undoubtedly because of their tremendous versatility. Incidentally, it was the Spaniards who introduced the chicken to the New World, although early records show that the Indians ate eggs from numerous types of other birds.

HUEVOS RANCHEROS

The sauce can be made in advance so breakfast or brunch is simply a matter of frying eggs—but what a way to serve them! See menu suggestion (page 229), for a traditional, wonderful brunch menu.

Yield: 4 servings

1 recipe Salsa Ranchero (page 58)
8 flour tortillas (1 for each plate plus 4 more to serve as bread)
8 eggs
1 cup grated Monterey Jack or sharp Cheddar cheese
3 tablespoons thinly sliced scallions, tops included
1 avocado, peeled and sliced in thin wedges
1 large tomato cut in wedges

1. Prepare sauce and keep it warm. Wrap tortillas in foil and heat in a 325°F oven for 15 minutes. Heat four serving plates in same oven.

2. Fry eggs sunny-side up or poach them.

3. Assemble Huevos Rancheros by placing a tortilla on each plate; then pour about ¼ cup sauce over and put 2 eggs on top. Sprinkle ¼ cup grated cheese and a few scallion slices over each serving. Place plates back in oven only long enough to melt the cheese, about 5 minutes.

4. Garnish each plate with avocado and tomato wedges. Serve remaining warm sauce and extra tortillas generously buttered with sweet butter and rolled separately.

NEW MEXICO TORTILLA DE PATATA

A Spanish potato omelet spiced southwestern style. In Spain the word *tortilla* refers to omelet-style eggs baked in the round. Sometimes called "tortilla de huevos."

Yield: 4 servings

3 tablespoons butter (or olive oil for a more traditional Spanish flavor)
1 large Spanish onion, chopped
1 clove garlic, minced
2 medium-size potatoes, thinly sliced
8 eggs
¼ cup water or beer
½ teaspoon salt
Freshly ground black pepper
¾ teaspoon ground pure mild red chile
4 mild green chiles, parched and peeled (page 13), sliced in thin rings
3 tablespoons butter (or olive oil)
1 cup coarsely grated Monterey Jack cheese
1 recipe Salsa Fresca (page 50)

1. Heat 3 tablespoons butter or oil in a large, heavy skillet. Sauté the onion and garlic until transluscent. Add the potatoes and cook until tender. Sprinkle with a little salt and pepper, remove from heat, and let cool for 5 to 10 minutes.

2. In a large mixing bowl, beat together the eggs, water or beer, salt, pepper, and ground chile. Stir in the green chiles and the potato mixture.

3. Heat 3 tablespoons more butter in the skillet, pour in the egg mixture, and, as it sets on the bottom, gently shake the pan and slide a spatula under to keep omelet from sticking to the bottom of pan.

4. When omelet is almost firm, cook the top of omelet in one of

the following two ways: a) place a plate on top of skillet and invert both so that the omelet is on the plate, bottom side up, and then slide back into the skillet to briefly cook the other side, or, b) place skillet under a preheated broiler about 4 inches from heat and broil until just set but not dry, about 2 or 3 minutes.

5. Serve immediately topped with the Monterey Jack cheese. Serve a side dish of Salsa Fresca.

HUEVOS SANTA FE

These eggs with Chile con Queso sauce are a special dish for any occasion. Serve with extra warmed wheat tortillas.

Yield: 4 servings

> 4 wheat flour or corn tortillas (plus extra for serving as bread)
> 3 tablespoons butter
> 1 small onion, chopped
> 6 green chiles, parched and peeled (page 13), cut in strips
> 3 tablespoons flour
> ½ teaspoon salt
> Freshly ground black pepper
> 2 cups milk
> ½ cup sharp Cheddar cheese, grated
> ½ cup Monterey Jack cheese, grated
> 1 teaspoon jalapeño juice, if desired
> 8 eggs
> 1 large ripe tomato, thinly sliced

1. Wrap tortillas in foil and heat in a 325°F oven for 15 minutes to soften. Heat four serving plates in same oven.

2. Melt butter in a saucepan. Sauté onion and green chiles until onion is tender; stir in flour, salt, and pepper. Gradually add the 2 cups of milk and cook and stir the sauce until smooth and

thickened. Add the cheese and stir until it is melted. Season with jalapeño juice, if desired. Keep warm.

3. Fry or poach the eggs.

4. Place a tortilla on each of the warm plates, top with tomato slices, 2 eggs per serving, and pour Chile con Queso sauce over. Serve immediately with a green vegetable such as broccoli or asparagus.

POTATOES AND CHORIZO WITH EGGS

A Mexican hash and eggs, this recipe makes a hearty and a rib-sticking brunch.

Yield: 4 servings

1 recipe Papas y Chorizo (page 188)
4 eggs
½ cup coarsely grated full cream sharp Cheddar cheese, optional

1. Prepare Papas y Chorizo according to the recipe.

2. While the hot potato mixture is still in the skillet, make four indentations in it and break an egg into each indentation. Cover the skillet and cook for about 5 minutes until the eggs are set.

3. Sprinkle with a bit of grated cheese for garnish, if desired.

CHILAQUILES Y HUEVOS

A hearty, flavorful way to salvage dried out corn tortillas or not-so-crisp tostadas.

Yield: 4 servings

2 tablespoons butter
1 medium-size onion, finely chopped
1 clove garlic, minced
3 tablespoons pure ground mild chile
½ teaspoon salt
¼ teaspoon ground comino
1 large tomato, sliced in thin wedges
¼ cup tomato juice
2 green chiles, finely chopped, or more to taste
3 cups crisp tostado pieces or torn corn tortilla pieces
8 eggs
¾ cup grated Monterey Jack cheese
¼ cup pitted black olive slices

1. Preheat oven to 350°F.
2. Heat 2 tablespoons butter in a saucepan and sauté the onion and garlic until onion is soft. Stir in the ground chile, salt, comino, tomato, tomato juice, and green chile. Simmer for about 5 minutes.
3. Stir the tostado pieces into the hot sauce, simmer 2 minutes, and pour all into a shallow oven-proof serving dish.
4. Poach or fry the eggs and arrange them on top of the chilaquiles. Sprinkle with the grated cheese.
5. Bake for about 10 minutes until cheese is melted. Garnish with the black olives and serve immediately.

CHORIZO "QUICHE"

A real taste treat. The fluted crust is very attractive, crisp, and delicious.

Yield: 6 servings

1 teaspoon butter or lard
Lard or oil for frying
1 wheat tortilla, 12-inch size (when making your own, use
   pieces of dough about the size of a tennis ball)
2 or 3 tablespoons tomato sauce mixed with ½ teaspoon
   jalapeño juice (or use red chile sauce or salsa verde if you
   have some on hand)
½ pound chorizo sausage
4 eggs
1 tablespoon minced fresh cilantro
1 cup light cream
½ teaspoon salt
Freshly ground black pepper to taste
1 cup grated Monterey Jack cheese
½ cup sliced scallions, tops included
1 small tomato, seeds gently squeezed out, chopped
   Salsa Fresca (page 50)

1. Butter a 9-inch pie plate with the 1 teaspoon butter; set aside. Fry tortilla in ¼ inch hot oil very briefly, being careful not to make it too crisp to fit into the pie plate. Fit the tortilla into the pie plate and brush with spicy tomato sauce mixture.

2. Remove the chorizo from casing, crumble, and fry until well browned; drain. Place in tortilla shell.

3. In a bowl, beat the eggs, cream, cilantro, salt, and pepper. Stir in the grated cheese, scallions, and tomato.

4. Pour egg mixture into tortilla shell and bake in a preheated 375°F oven for about 30 minutes, until the eggs are set.

5. Serve with Salsa Fresca.

VARIATION: Other meats, sauces, and combinations are also excellent—try crabmeat or chicken with eggs and green chiles, garnished with sour cream.

CRABMEAT AND AVOCADO OMELET

Yield: 4 servings

1 cup cooked crabmeat or small shrimp
Salsa Verde (page 56)
1 large avocado
8 eggs
⅓ cup light cream
½ teaspoon salt
Generous grinding of whole black peppercorns
¼ cup very thinly sliced scallions
3 tablespoons butter
½ cup sour cream

1. Mix the crabmeat with 3 tablespoons of the Salsa Verde; set aside. Peel and slice the avocado into thin strips.

2. Beat together the eggs, cream, salt, pepper, and scallions.

3. Heat 3 tablespoons butter in a heavy skillet; add the egg mixture, and, using a spatula, gently lift edges allowing uncooked eggs to flow into contact with the center of pan. When eggs are barely set, arrange the crabmeat and half of the avocado slices over half the omelet. Cover pan and heat for about 1 minute.

4. Fold the unfilled half of the omelet over the crabmeat and avocado and slide onto a warmed serving platter. Garnish with remaining avocado slices and dollops of sour cream, and serve immediately with extra Salsa Verde on the side.

ADDITIONAL SUGGESTIONS FOR HUEVOS

Warm tortillas topped with Carne Adobada (page 163) and eggs

Browned chorizo sausage and eggs scrambled together

Chile Beef (pages 131–36) and eggs

Omelet filled with spicy Guacamole (page 26) and melted Monterey Jack cheese, topped with sour cream and thin tomato wedges

Crisp-fried tortillas (Tostados, page 99) topped with frijoles refritos, eggs, and Salsa Fresca (page 50)

Assorted taco and tortilla fillings throughout this book used as fillings for omelets

When combined with chiles or chile-spiced meat or sauce, scrambled eggs make a terrific burrito or taco.

Carne (Beef)

A love for the taste of beef runs throughout the Southwest, and it is undoubtedly served more than any other meat.

BERNALILLO BEEF AND VEGETABLE STEW

This savory combination of local produce over rice is typically New Mexican. Simple to prepare, it has a super flavor, especially when complemented with wheat tortillas for sopping up the juice. The stew can be frozen for up to 8 months.

Yield: 4 to 6 servings

> 3 tablespoons lard or bacon drippings
> 2½ pounds stewing beef, cut in 1½-inch cubes
> ¼ cup flour
> 1 large onion, coarsely chopped
> 2 cloves garlic, minced
> 2 teaspoons fresh cilantro or parsley, minced
> 3 large ripe tomatoes, peeled and chopped
> Water
> 4 green chiles, parched and peeled (page 13), chopped
> Salt and freshly ground black pepper to taste
> 3 medium-size zucchini, sliced, each about 8 inches in length
>   (or substitute other vegetables such as green bell peppers,
>   carrots, or green beans)
> 4 cups cooked rice, optional

1. Heat lard or bacon drippings in a large, heavy skillet. Dredge the stewing beef in the flour and brown well.

2. Add the onion and garlic to the beef and cook until the onion begins to soften. Add the cilantro, tomatoes, 1 cup of water, the chopped chiles, and salt and pepper. Cover the skillet and simmer until meat is tender, about 1 hour, adding a little more water, if necessary.

3. Add the zucchini slices and simmer gently, covered, for about 10 minutes or until they are tender but not falling apart. Serve piping hot with rice.

CALABACITAS WITH BEEF

This New Mexican combination of beef and zucchini is an excellent choice for guests or for a family dinner. I always remember how well Jo Hubber made it for our many happy outings with the Albuquerque Pilot Club. She and her husband, Joe, were quite famous for preparing it as soon as the summer green chile harvest began. As with the other native chile stews, try serving with steaming, buttered wheat tortillas. Appropriate as both a side dish or a main course, this recipe can be frozen for up to 8 months.

Yield: 6 to 8 servings

¼ cup butter or bacon drippings
2½ pounds round steak sliced into *thin* strips, about 2 inches long
2 cloves garlic, minced
1 medium-size onion, thinly sliced and separated into rings
4 medium-size zucchini, sliced ⅜-inch thick
1 teaspoon salt
¼ teaspoon Mexican oregano
½ teaspoon ground comino
1 cup chopped freshly parched green chiles (see parching instructions, page 13)
1½ cups corn kernels, fresh or frozen
¾ cup grated full cream sharp Cheddar cheese

1. Heat butter or bacon drippings over high heat in a large, heavy skillet. Add beef slices and brown quickly, but well. Remove to a plate.

2. Sauté garlic, onion, and zucchini in same skillet until zucchini is crisp-tender.

3. Stir in the browned beef and heat for about 5 minutes. Stir in the grated cheese and serve as soon as the cheese has melted.

MEATLOAF SOUTHWESTERN STYLE

There's a surprise inside this spicy loaf. Serve with hot red or green chile sauce or Salsa Fresca (pages 50–55).

Yield: 6 servings

2 pounds ground beef (or 1 pound each of ground beef and fresh ground pork)
2 slices bread, cubed, moistened with water, and water squeezed out
1 large onion, finely chopped
2 eggs
2 cloves garlic, minced
2 teaspoons pure ground mild red chile
1½ teaspoons salt
½ teaspoon ground Mexican oregano
⅛ teaspoon ground comino
2 or 3 mild green chiles, parched and peeled (page 13), chopped
⅓ cup tomato sauce
1½ cups grated Monterey Jack cheese
1 large ripe avocado, peeled, pitted, and sliced in wedges
Salsa of your choice (pages 49–61)

1. In a large mixing bowl, combine all ingredients except the cheese and the avocado.
2. Place half the mixture in a loaf or 1½-quart baking pan, indent slightly lengthwise down the center allowing a 1-inch margin all around, and place 1 cup of the grated cheese and the avocado slices on it. Top with remaining meat loaf mixture and press the edges together to seal. Sprinkle the remaining ½ cup of cheese on top of meatloaf.
3. Bake at 350°F for 1¼ to 1½ hours, or until done.

VARIATION: Prepare as individual single serving-size meat loaves, and bake for 30 to 45 minutes or cook on an outdoor grill.

Because of the avocado hidden in the center, it is not recommended that these servings be frozen.

POT ROAST NEW MEXICO

Pot roast with a Tex-Mex twist. To enjoy every last drop of the excellent sauce, serve with a big basket of warmed wheat tortillas!

This pot roast can be frozen for up to 8 months in the marinade before cooking. To cook, simply remove from the freezer, place in a 350°F oven, and bake, covered, for about 2½ hours. Any leftover marinade can be frozen for later use.

Yield: 6 to 8 servings

> 3 pounds beef chuck or round steak, about 2 inches thick
> 1½ cups dry white wine
> 3 tablespoons wine vinegar
> 4 mild green chiles, parched and peeled (page 13), chopped
> 3 tablespoons brown sugar
> 1½ teaspoons salt
> 2 cloves garlic, finely minced
> 3 tablespoons lard or bacon drippings
> 1 large onion, sliced into thin rings
> ¾ cup beef bouillon or broth
> 3 tablespoons tomato paste

1. Place beef in a shallow flat-bottomed pan just large enough to hold the meat. Combine the wine, vinegar, chiles, brown sugar, salt, and garlic to make a marinade. Pour over the beef, turn the meat over to coat evenly. Marinate the meat in the refrigerator overnight, turning at least 2 or 3 times and spooning sauce over top.

2. The next day, drain the meat and reserve the marinade. Heat the lard or bacon drippings in a large, heavy skillet or Dutch oven and brown the meat thoroughly on both sides. Add 1½ cups of the reserved marinade, the onion, bouillon, and tomato paste.

3. Cover the pan and simmer the pot roast for about 1½ to 2 hours, or until tender. Remove the cover and simmer a little longer, if necessary, to reduce and thicken the sauce.

4. Serve pot roast on a heated platter topped with some of the sauce. Serve the remaining sauce separately. Garnish with parsley and tomatoes.

CARNE ASADA (MARINATED GRILLED STEAK)

Inspired by south-of-the-border braseros! Serve as a London broil-type steak with salad and vegetables or as the filling for soft tacos. The cooked steak can be frozen for up to 8 months.

Yield: 10 servings

    3 or 4 pounds beef loin or filet
    1 medium-size onion, finely chopped
    1 tablespoon olive oil
    ¾ cup red wine vinegar
    ½ teaspoon salt
    ½ teaspoon each of pepper, pure ground red chile, ground
        Mexican oregano, comino, cloves, and cinnamon
    2 cloves garlic, minced
    12 hot wheat tortillas, optional
    Salsa Colorado (page 54) or Salsa Fresca (page 50), optional

1. Place the steak in a large, shallow flat-bottomed dish.

2. In a saucepan, sauté the onion in the olive oil until it begins to soften. Add remaining ingredients and simmer the marinade, covered, for 10 minutes. Cool.

3. Pour cooled marinade over steak, turn the steak over to coat evenly, and let set at room temperature for 2 hours.

4. Grill on an outdoor grill, preferably charring outside and leaving inside rare, basting as the meat cooks. Thinly slice and serve as is or place a few strips in each wheat tortilla; top with salsa and roll.

VARIATION: Marinate large chunks of beef, skewer them with fresh vegetables for kabobs, and grill.

CARNE DESHEBRADA (SHREDDED BEEF)

Simple yet substantial, this flavorful meat dish has many uses. By merely altering the amount of liquid used in cooking, you can prepare an excellent main dish topping for rice and beans, or fillings for tacos, burritos, taquitos, and empanadas. It will keep frozen for up to 6 months.

Yield: 6 servings

2 cups water
1 teaspoon salt
1½ pounds beef chuck
3 tablespoons lard or bacon drippings
1 onion, cut in half and sliced into thin half rings
2 cloves garlic, minced
1 tablespoon flour
3 medium-size tomatoes, finely chopped
1 jalapeño chile (or less), minced
3 medium-size green bell peppers, sliced thinly in strips
Freshly ground black pepper

1. Place water and salt in a 3-quart saucepan; add the meat, bring to a boil, reduce the heat, cover, and simmer until meat is very tender, about 1½ hours. Drain the meat and reserve the broth.
2. Using two forks, shred the beef.
3. In a large, heavy skillet, heat the lard and sauté the onion and garlic; stir in the flour, add the tomatoes, and simmer for about 10 minutes or until tomatoes are soft. Add the jalapeño, the bell pepper strips, the black pepper, the shredded beef, and ¾ cup of the reserved beef broth. Cover and simmer until bell pepper is soft. Taste and adjust seasonings.

VARIATIONS: For meat and vegetables in one dish, add a sliced fresh zucchini or a cup of peas when you put in the bell pepper.

Or, omit tomatoes and bell pepper for taquito or empanada fillings.

PICADILLO

A true Texas inspiration and what a treat! Serve as a main course in a crisp corn tortilla taco or a soft wheat tortilla rolled into a taco (see pages 83–97). Serve with rice, fresh fruit, and vegetable. Picadillo can be frozen for 2 months.

Yield: 6 servings

> 2 tablespoons lard or bacon drippings
> 1½ pounds lean beef chuck, coarsely chopped
> 2 cloves garlic, minced
> 1 large onion, chopped
> 1½ teaspoons salt
> 1½ teaspoons sugar
> 1½ teaspoons ground cinnamon
> ½ teaspoon ground comino
> ¼ teaspoon ground cloves
> 3 tablespoons vinegar
> ⅔ cup raisins
> ¼ cup water
> 3 large, ripe tomatoes, peeled and chopped (or use 1½ cups canned)
> ¾ cup slivered almonds, toasted

1. Heat the lard in a skillet; add the beef and brown well. Add the garlic and onion and cook until onion begins to soften.
2. Add all other ingredients except the almonds and simmer, covered, for about 40 minutes or until beef is very tender.
3. Place picadillo on a serving plate or in taco shells or warm wheat tortillas, garnish with the slivered almonds, and serve with rice, fresh fruit salad, and a vegetable.

VARIATION: Pork cut in ½-inch cubes is a very tasty substitute.

Puerco (Pork)

Introduced to the New World by the conquistadors and readily accepted by the Indians, pork today is an integral part of southwestern and Mexican cooking. Pork, or puerco, possesses a special quality which is greatly complemented by chiles, lending itself fabulously to a multitude of wonderful dishes, each tastefully different from the next.

PORK WITH CHILE VERDE

Senator Joe Montoyo from New Mexico was famous for this stew. He won the Capitol chile cook-off more than once with the recipe. Absolutely critical: You must serve wheat tortillas on the side for scooping up the great sauce! The stew may be frozen for up to 3 months.

Yield: 4 servings

2 pounds boneless pork, cut in 1-inch cubes
3 tablespoons flour
2 tablespoons lard or bacon drippings
1 large onion, chopped
2 cloves garlic, minced
Water
1 teaspoon salt
Freshly ground black pepper
½ teaspoon ground Mexican oregano
¼ teaspoon ground comino
3 large ripe tomatoes, peeled and chopped
20 fresh green chiles, parched and peeled (page 13), chopped

1. Sprinkle pork cubes with flour. Heat lard in a large, heavy skillet or saucepan and brown pork. Remove to a plate.
2. Sauté onion and garlic in the same pan until onion is soft. Return meat to the pan.
3. Add water to just barely cover the meat. Add salt, pepper, Mexican oregano, and comino. Cover and simmer for 1 hour.
4. Add the tomatoes and green chiles; simmer 30 minutes or longer, adding a little more water if necessary, until flavors are well blended.

CARNE ADOBADA (PORK IN CHILE MARINADE)

Delicious and easy to make, carne adobada will get raves from everyone! Serve with wheat tortillas, sopaipillas or cornbread, a fresh green salad and refritos topped with cheese. Or use as a super filling for spicy burritos or tacos! The pork can be frozen in the marinade for up to 3 months or you can freeze any leftover marinade separately for later use.

Yield: 10 to 12 servings

1 cup chile caribe (page 53)
4 cups water
2 teaspoons salt
4 cloves garlic, chopped
2 tablespoons ground Mexican oregano
2 tablespoons ground comino
5 pounds loin or shoulder pork chops, sliced 1 inch thick and trimmed of excess fat

1. Place all ingredients except pork in a blender container; process for a few seconds until sauce is thoroughly mixed.

2. Lay pork slices in a large flat baking dish; pour sauce over and turn the meat slices to coat them evenly. Marinate overnight, or for at least 10 hours, in the refrigerator.

3. Bake, covered, at 325°F for 30 minutes. Remove cover from baking dish, spoon sauce over top, and bake for 30 minutes longer, basting occasionally.

PORK LOIN IN SALSA VERDE

Great company fare—elegant, easy, and sumptuous. Leftovers may be frozen for up to 3 months.

Yield: 8 servings

1 boneless pork roast (4 pounds, loin or butt), tied
½ teaspoon ground Mexican oregano
⅛ teaspoon thyme
Salt and freshly ground black pepper

1 large tomato, peeled and cut in chunks
1 can (10 ounces) tomatillos, drained
4 green chiles, parched and peeled (page 13)
1 onion, coarsely chopped
1 clove garlic
1 tablespoon minced parsley or fresh cilantro
2 tablespoons lard or bacon drippings
1 cup chicken or beef broth, approximately
Salt
Freshly ground black pepper

1. Place roast in a baking pan and sprinkle with oregano, thyme, salt, and pepper. Bake at 350°F for about 2½ hours or until meat thermometer reads 170°F.

2. While roast is baking, prepare the sauce: place tomato, tomatillos, chiles, onion, garlic, and parsley in blender or food processor container. Process until smooth.

3. Heat the lard or bacon drippings in a heavy skillet. Add the puree and fry for 3 to 4 minutes, stirring constantly. Add the broth and salt and pepper to taste. The sauce should be the consistency of heavy cream; thin with a little more broth, if necessary.

4. When roast is done, slice and arrange on a warmed serving platter. Pour the heated sauce over the sliced roast and serve.

NOTE: For ease in dinner preparation, cook the roast and make the sauce earlier in the day. Slice, arrange on an oven-proof serving platter, pour the sauce over, and cover with a lid or foil. Warm, covered, in oven before serving—this incorporates the sauce flavor into the meat.

PUERCO DE MOLE (PORK IN MOLE SAUCE)

Delicious, different, and spicy, Puerco de Mole is wonderful served with rice, avocado vinaigrette salad or guacamole, wheat tortillas, and icy cold beer. Leftovers may be frozen for up to 3 months and make terrific tacos.

Yield: 6 to 8 servings

2 pounds boneless pork
2½ cups water
1 bay leaf
½ jalapeño chile, or more depending on preference
1 slice bread or ½ of a wheat flour tortilla
1 medium-size tomato, peeled
1 clove garlic
¼ teaspoon cinnamon
⅛ teaspoon ground cloves
¼ teaspoon freshly ground black pepper
2 tablespoons lard
½ teaspoon salt, or to taste

1. Trim fat from meat and cut into 1-inch cubes or thin strips. Place in a saucepan with 2½ cups water and the bay leaf. Bring to a boil, skim foam from surface, cover, and simmer about 30 minutes or until meat is tender. Drain meat, reserving the broth.
2. In a blender or food processor container, place the jalapeño chile, the bread or tortilla, tomato, garlic, cinnamon, cloves, and pepper. Puree, adding reserved broth one tablespoon at a time, if necessary, to achieve a medium consistency puree.
3. Heat 2 tablespoons lard in a large, heavy skillet, add the

mole puree, and sauté, stirring constantly, for 2 or 3 minutes. Mixture will be very pasty.

4. Add the meat, stir to coat it, and then add 1 cup of the reserved broth. Cook and stir until sauce is smooth and thickened, at least 30 minutes. Add salt and adjust seasonings. If sauce is too thick, add a little more broth to thin it.

SOUTHWESTERN COUNTRY RIBS

These snappy, border-style ribs are excellent for casual outdoor summer entertaining. If by some chance there are leftovers, they can be frozen for up to 3 months.

Yield: 4 servings

6 tablespoons olive oil
¼ cup red wine vinegar
1½ teaspoons salt
¼ teaspoon, or more, piquín quebrado
2 teaspoons ground Mexican oregano
3 large cloves garlic, finely minced
2 pounds country style ribs, or 3 pounds lean spareribs
2 cups Red Chile Sauce (page 52), hot or mild, your preference
1 medium-size onion, finely chopped

1. Place oil, vinegar, salt, pepper, oregano, and garlic in a jar; cover and shake the marinade.

2. Lay the ribs in a baking dish which closely fits the ribs laid in a single layer. Pour the marinade over and allow to marinate for 2 to 3 hours at room temperature.

3. Pour the Red Chile Sauce over the ribs, sprinkle with the chopped onion, and bake in a 350°F oven for 1½ to 2 hours, or until done.

Pesca (Fish and Seafood)

Fish and shellfish are delectably enhanced by the seasonings and spices of the cuisine of the Southwest. Basically, all the recipes included in this chapter are of Mexican origin. All seafood loses flavor and texture when frozen; it is best when purchased fresh and served the same day.

SHRIMP IN NUT SAUCE

Prepare this spicy, intriguing sauce in advance so that you can be a guest at your own party!

Yield: 4 servings

⅔ cup sunflower seeds (raw or roasted)
2 cloves garlic, chopped
1 tablespoon pure ground mild red chile (or adjust to taste with a little pure ground hot chile)
½ teaspoon coriander seeds
1 tablespoon fresh minced cilantro, optional
2 large ripe tomatoes, peeled and chopped (about 1¼ cups)
3 tablespoons olive oil
1¼ pounds shelled and deveined shrimp, lightly sprinkled with salt
1 medium-size onion, finely chopped
¾ cup chicken broth, approximately
Juice of ½ lime
½ teaspoon salt
Freshly ground black pepper
3 cups hot cooked white rice
Parsley or fresh cilantro for garnish

1. Place sunflower seeds, garlic, chile, coriander seeds, cilantro, and tomatoes in blender jar. Process until smooth.

2. In a large, heavy skillet, heat olive oil until hot; stir and fry the shrimp until cooked, only about 3 or 4 minutes. Remove from skillet and keep warm.

3. Sauté the chopped onion in the remaining oil until translucent. With skillet on medium high heat, add the puree to the onions and cook, stirring constantly, for 2 to 3 minutes. Add broth, lime juice, and salt and pepper to taste. Sauce should be the consistency of heavy cream. If it is too thick, thin by adding a bit more chicken broth. Adjust seasonings, adding more ground chile, if desired.

4. Place rice around sides of a warmed serving platter. Put hot shrimp in the center and pour the sauce over. Garnish with snipped parsley or cilantro and serve.

BAKED FILET OF COD TOPPED WITH LEMON, CHILE CARIBE, AND OLIVE OIL

Yield: 6 servings

6 large-size fillets of cod fish (or any other firm, white fish
    such as snapper, sea bass, and halibut)
Flour
¼ cup olive oil
2 tablespoons melted butter
2 tablespoons finely chopped scallions
1 tablespoon chopped fresh coriander (optional)
2 teaspoons freshly squeezed lemon juice
3 tablespoons minced fresh parsley
2 tablespoons Chile Caribe (page 53)
½ teaspoon salt
¼ teaspoon freshly ground black pepper
1 fresh lemon, thinly sliced

1. Very lightly dust the fish filets with flour. Place them in a single layer in a buttered baking pan (preferably one suitable for serving).

2. Place all other ingredients except lemon slices in a jar; shake well to combine. Pour evenly over fish.

3. Bake in a preheated 375°F oven for 20 minutes. Arrange lemon slices over filets and return to oven for 5 minutes longer, until fish tests done by flaking easily with a fork.

SEAFOOD BROCHETTE CAMPECHE STYLE

Fruits of the sea from the gulf coast region of Campeche, Mexico. Serve with crusty bolillos, your favorite green salad, and Mexican rice.

Yield: 8 to 10 servings

½ pound king crab meat or lump crab meat
½ pound cod fillet, cut in 1½-inch pieces
½ pound sea scallops, cut in half if very large
½ pound large shrimp, peeled and deveined
2 green or red sweet bell peppers, cut in 1½-inch pieces
1 bunch large plump scallions (Use 2 or 3 pieces, 1½ inches each, from the base end of each scallion. Reserve the tops for the marinade.)

---

5 tablespoons fresh lemon juice
2 tablespoons fresh lime juice
¼ cup dry white wine
½ cup very finely chopped scallion tops
½ cup olive oil
3 cloves garlic, very finely minced
1 small ripe tomato, very finely chopped
¾ teaspoon salt
¾ teaspoon ground Mexican oregano
1 tablespoon ground pure mild red chile
Salsa of your choice, optional (see pages 49–61)

1. Put a combination of crab, cod, scallops, shrimp, green or red pepper, and scallion pieces on each of eight or ten skewers. Place filled skewers in a large, shallow, flat dish.

2. Prepare marinade by combining the remaining ingredients in a jar. Shake well and pour over the skewered seafood. Marinate in refrigerator for at least 4 hours, turning occasionally. Reserve marinade.

3. Preheat broiler and broil seafood 5 inches from heat for 5 to 7 minutes on each side, or until opaque and firm to the touch. Do not overcook.

4. Place brochettes on a large, warmed serving platter and pour reserved marinade over. Garnish with thin lime and lemon slices and serve with rice, a fresh green salad, and hot, crusty bolillos (pages 198–99). Serve with a table sauce, if desired.

NOTE: These are also fantastic when cooked over coals on the grill.

ENSENADA SHRIMP

A wonderful blending of garlic, lime juice, and caribe chile makes any occasion a special one.

Yield: 4 to 5 servings

1½ pounds fresh large shrimp
6 tablespoons butter
⅓ cup olive oil
1 large clove garlic, very finely minced
2 tablespoons Chile Caribe (page 53) or 2½ teaspoons ground mild red chile
2 tablespoons freshly squeezed lime juice
2 tablespoons finely chopped scallions
½ teaspoon salt
Freshly ground black pepper

1. Shell the shrimp, being careful not to remove the last small segment of shell or the tail. With a small, sharp knife, slit each shrimp down the back to butterfly, and remove the vein. Wash shrimp quickly under cold water and drain on paper towelling.

2. In a shallow, flameproof baking dish or pan just large enough to hold the shrimp in a single layer, heat the butter and olive oil over medium heat. Add the garlic and sauté until garlic is slightly cooked. Remove from heat and stir in the chile caribe,

lime juice, scallions, salt, and a little freshly ground pepper. Preheat broiler to its highest heat.

3. Add the shrimp to the pan and turn them to coat thoroughly. Broil 4 to 5 inches from heat for 5 minutes; then turn the shrimp over and broil another 5 to 10 minutes or until lightly browned and slightly firm. Be careful not to overcook them.

4. Arrange cooked shrimp on a serving platter (if one was not used for cooking), pour sauce over, garnish with fresh lime slices or wedges, and serve.

YUCATECAN SHRIMP AND CRAB

Superb, simple, and somewhat tropical.

Yield: 4 servings

2 tablespoons olive oil
3 tablespoons butter
2 tablespoons finely minced shallots
1 large clove garlic, finely minced
½ pound fresh shelled shrimp, deveined
½ pound fresh lump crabmeat
3 large ripe tomatoes, peeled and chopped
3 or 4 green chiles, parched and peeled (page 13), chopped
1½ teaspoons freshly squeezed lime juice
½ teaspoon minced fresh basil or ¼ teaspoon dried
Salt
Freshly ground black pepper
3 scallions, sliced in half lengthwise, then cut into 1-inch pieces
Avocado slices that have been sprinkled with lime juice

1. Heat olive oil and butter in a large, heavy skillet; sauté the shallots and garlic until they just barely begin to brown. Add the shrimp and crabmeat and sauté, stirring gently, for about 2 minutes.

2. Add the tomatoes, chopped green chiles, lime juice, basil,

salt, and pepper. Cover and simmer for 5 minutes. Add scallions, cover, and simmer 3 minutes longer.

3. Place on a warmed serving platter and garnish with avocado slices.

HUACHINANGO EN SALSA
(RED SNAPPER IN GREEN SAUCE)

Yield: 6 servings

2½ pounds red snapper fillets
Salt
Flour
¼ cup olive oil
2 cloves garlic, minced
1 large onion, chopped
2 tablespoons minced cilantro (optional)
1 can (10 ounces) Mexican tomatillos, undrained
2 large ripe tomatoes, peeled and chopped
2 jalapeño chiles, seeded and chopped
¼ cup minced fresh parsley
¼ teaspoon freshly ground black pepper
12 pitted black olives, sliced

1. Season fish fillets with salt and sprinkle with flour. Heat olive oil in a large, heavy skillet and cook the fish on both sides until tender and golden brown. Remove to a serving platter and keep warm.

2. Sauté the garlic and onion in the same skillet; then add the cilantro, tomatillos and their liquid, tomatoes, jalapeño chiles, parsley, and pepper. Cook the sauce over medium heat until it reaches a medium consistency, about 5 to 10 minutes.

3. Pour sauce over fish on platter, garnish with sliced black olives, and serve at once.

Pollo (Poultry)

Poultry is extremely popular in southwestern kitchens; its mild, subtly flavored flesh lends itself to limitless variations. I've included recipes for poultry simmered in robust sauces, for spicy chile concoctions, for mild, delicate chicken in cream, and, of course, for the famed mole poblano from Old Mexico.

MOLE POBLANO DE GUAJOLOTE (TURKEY IN MOLE POBLANO)

The turkey, or guajolote, is native to the Americas. Mole poblano is a traditional Mexican dish dating back to early colonial times, reputedly having been created by a nun in a convent in Puebla, Mexico. This "national dish of Mexico" is delicious served with rice, frijoles, guacamole or avocado, and tomato vinaigrette, and fresh hot tortillas or bolillos. It can be frozen for up to 6 months.

Yield: 6 servings

1 turkey breast, about 3 pounds, cut in serving-size pieces
2 turkey thighs, about 3 pounds total, cut in serving-size
   pieces
Water
1 carrot, cut in 1-inch pieces
1 small onion, halved
1 bay leaf
¾ teaspoon salt
8 whole black peppercorns
1 recipe Mole Sauce (page 61)
1 tablespoon toasted sesame seeds (Chicken with Chile-Nut
   Mole)

1. Place turkey breast and thigh pieces in a large pot and cover with enough water to just cover. Add the carrot, onion, bay leaf, salt, and peppercorns. Bring to a boil, cover, and simmer until tender, about 1¼ hours. Drain and reserve broth.

2. While turkey is simmering, prepare Mole Sauce (page 61) in a large, heavy skillet, using the turkey broth to prepare it.

3. Place the cooked, drained turkey pieces in the skillet with the mole, turning to coat evenly. Cover and simmer for 30 minutes, adding a bit more broth if sauce becomes too thick. Taste and adjust seasonings.

4. Remove to a deep serving platter, sprinkle with toasted sesame seeds, and serve.

NOTE: To prepare a larger company dish using 1 whole small turkey (about 7 or 8 pounds) or 2 chickens (about 4 pounds each), triple the Mole Sauce recipe.

CHICKEN WITH CHILE-NUT MOLE

Ground seeds and tortillas are the thickeners for the sauce in this recipe. Subtly spiced, this entree was great fun to develop and test, on both adults and children—it gets rave reviews every time! It can be frozen for up to 6 months.

Yield: 6 to 8 servings

2 frying chickens (about 3 pounds each), cut in pieces
Water
1½ teaspoons salt
10 whole black peppercorns
2 bay leaves

½ cup sesame seeds, toasted*
¾ cup hulled sunflower or pumpkin seeds, toasted*
1 tablespoon bacon drippings or lard
2 corn tortillas, torn in pieces
Reserved chicken broth
1 to 2 tablespoons pure ground mild red chile
2 green chiles or more, parched, peeled, and chopped (page 13)

---

2 tablespoons bacon drippings or lard
1 onion, chopped
¾ teaspoon salt

1. Place chicken pieces in a large pot; add water to barely cover; add salt, peppercorns, and bay leaves. Bring to a boil;

cover and simmer until tender but still firm, about 25 minutes. Drain, reserving broth.

2. While chicken is simmering, prepare the mole: Toast the seeds and place in blender or food processor container. Heat 1 tablespoon drippings in a large, heavy skillet and fry the torn tortilla pieces until browned. Add to the blender container. Add about ¾ cup chicken broth, the ground chile, and the green chiles. Process until very smooth and pasty, gradually adding more broth if mixture is too thick to process.

3. Heat 2 tablespoons drippings in the skillet and sauté the chopped onion over high heat until lightly browned. With heat still high, add the mole and cook, stirring constantly, for about 2 minutes. Stir in ¾ teaspoon salt and 1½ cups chicken broth. Add more broth if needed to thin sauce to a medium consistency. Taste and adjust seasonings.

4. Place chicken pieces in the sauce, turning to coat them evenly. Cover and simmer 15 minutes or until hot.

---

* Toast seeds in a 300°F oven for 10 to 15 minutes or until slightly golden, or toast in a dry skillet over high heat, stirring constantly. Remove as soon as they begin to brown.

NOTE: If a spicier mole is desired, add more green or red chiles to taste.

POLLO EN MOLE VERDE
(CHICKEN IN GREEN CHILE SAUCE)

A "south-of-the-border" inspiration, this version is somewhat lighter than the traditional mole. Serve with rice, tortillas, and your favorite salad. Leftovers, which can be frozen for up to 6 months, are great in tacos and burritos.

Yield: 3 to 4 servings

1 frying chicken (3 to 4 pounds), cut up
2 cups water
1/2 teaspoon salt
1 cup pumpkin seeds
1 clove garlic, minced
1 recipe Salsa Verde Mexican-Style (page 56)
1 tablespoon lard or bacon drippings
Salt
Freshly ground black pepper

1. Place chicken in a large, heavy skillet with 2 cups water and 1/2 teaspoon salt. Bring to a boil, cover and reduce heat, and simmer until tender, about 35 minutes. Drain chicken, reserving the broth, and remove from the skillet.

2. Prepare the mole by grinding the pumpkin seeds in a blender; then add the garlic and Salsa Verde. Puree until smooth.

3. Over moderately high heat, heat the 1 tablespoon lard in the skillet, add the mole puree, and cook, stirring constantly, for 2 to 3 minutes. Thin to a medium consistency by adding small amounts of the reserved chicken broth. Taste and season with salt and freshly ground pepper.

4. Return the chicken pieces to the skillet, turning to coat them evenly with the mole. Cover and simmer, without boiling, until hot, about 15 minutes.

CHICKEN AND CHORIZO

A subtle, Spanish-inspired dish, it will freeze well for up to 6 months.

Yield: 4 to 6 servings

3 tablespoons lard or bacon drippings
1 large frying chicken (about 4 pounds), cut up
2 or 3 chorizo sausages, sliced
2 medium-size onions, thinly sliced and separated into rings
2 cloves garlic, minced
2 large ripe tomatoes, chopped
1 tablespoon fresh cilantro, minced (optional)
1 teaspoon salt
¼ teaspoon freshly ground black pepper
1 to 2 jalapeño chiles (or to taste), finely chopped

1. Heat lard in a large skillet and brown the chicken. Remove to a plate.
2. In the same skillet, cook the sausage slices until browned; remove from skillet.
3. Sauté the onion rings and garlic in the remaining fat until onions are soft and lightly browned. Add the tomatoes, cilantro, salt, pepper, and jalapeños to taste. Cook and stir for about 5 minutes. The sauce should be of medium consistency; if it is too thick, add a little chicken broth.
4. Return chicken and chorizo to skillet, turning pieces to coat with the sauce. Cover and simmer until tender, about 30 minutes.

Vegetables and Side Dishes

The list of vegetables native to the New World is lengthy: sweet bell peppers, tomatoes, squash (both summer and winter varieties), potatoes, chayote, green and wax beans, pumpkins, corn . . . to say nothing of the controversial chile, which is related to the eggplant and potato, yet botanically is classified as a fruit.

Undoubtedly, the most often served vegetables are beans and rice. In southwestern cooking, fresh corn and posole (corn hominy), potatoes, zucchini, tomatoes, and chiles are also used in abundance.

Green vegetables lend themselves to endless intriguing flavor combinations using the spices and seasonings of the southwestern kitchen.

FRIJOLES (BASIC MEXICAN BEANS)

In Mexico and the Southwest, beans are often served two or three meals a day. Very nutritious and delicious, they provide an excellent source of protein at a very economical price. Slow cooking and the addition of flavorful fat, such as bacon fat, lard, or meat drippings of any kind, bring out the full, rich flavor of frijoles. Although many varieties of beans can be used, the most popular variety in the southwestern diet is the pinto bean. They can be served with almost any meal as a side dish or as a main course with a chile meat sauce spooned over and with sopaipillas or tortillas for a complete meal.

Frijoles can be stored in a sealed container and frozen for up to 1 year.

Yield: 3 1/2 cups

> 2 cups (1 pound) dried pinto beans
> 5 cups water, or more
> 1 large clove garlic, minced
> 1 1/2 teaspoons salt
> 1/4 cup bacon drippings or 1/2 cup cubed salt pork

1. Rinse and sort beans; cover with water and soak overnight. Drain; add the 5 cups water, adding more as needed; bring to a boil, reduce heat, and simmer for 30 minutes.

2. Add the garlic, salt, and bacon drippings. If using salt pork, do not add salt until beans are fully cooked. Simmer until tender, about 2 1/2 to 3 hours, adding more water as necessary. Taste and adjust seasonings. The beans should be very soft.

FRIJOLES REFRITOS (REFRIED BEANS)

A basic and much loved staple throughout the Southwest and Mexico. Serve with salsa, if desired, as a side dish, and use them abundantly in tacos, burritos, nacho platters, enchiladas, and tostadas. They can be frozen for up to 6 months.

Yield: 6 to 8 servings

1 tablespoon (or more) bacon drippings or lard
2 cloves garlic, finely minced
2 tablespoons finely chopped onion
4 cups cooked pinto beans (use canned if you haven't the time to cook dry beans)
Salt to taste
1 cup grated Monterey Jack or Cheddar cheese

1. Heat the bacon drippings in a heavy skillet over medium heat. Add the garlic and onion, and cook until onion is transluscent; then add beans with a little of the liquid and mash them well, adding additional drippings as desired. Salt to taste.

2. Fry over medium heat for about 15 minutes, turning to prevent burning, until they reach a thick, pastelike consistency.

3. Top with grated cheese and serve piping hot. Place under the broiler briefly to thoroughly melt the cheese, if desired.

MEXICAN FRIED RICE

With its wonderful flavor, and its ease of preparation, Mexican rice adds a special touch to any meal. It can be frozen for up to 3 months.

Yield: 4 servings

> 1 cup uncooked long-grain white rice
> 3 tablespoons lard or bacon fat
> 1 medium-size onion, chopped
> 1 clove garlic, minced
> 1 large tomato, peeled and chopped
> 2 cups chicken broth (or 1 cup water and 1 cup broth)
> ½ teaspoon salt

1. Rinse the rice in cold water; drain. Repeat. Drain thoroughly.
2. In a heavy skillet, heat the lard or bacon fat and sauté the onion and garlic until onion is golden. Remove to a plate. In the same skillet, sauté the raw rice until golden.
3. Return the onion and garlic to the pan with the browned rice; add the tomato, chicken broth, and salt. Bring to a boil, reduce heat to very low, cover, and simmer for 20 minutes *without* lifting the lid.

VARIATION: For spicy rice, add with the liquid a finely minced jalapeño chile or pure ground hot or mild red chile to taste.

ARROZ Y VERDURAS (RICE AND VEGETABLES)

Colorful and with a hint of chile. It can be frozen for up to 3 months.

Yield: 6 servings

1 cup uncooked long-grain rice
3 tablespoons lard or bacon fat
1 large clove garlic, minced
1 medium-size onion, chopped
1 medium-size carrot, shredded
½ cup uncooked peas
1 medium-size tomato, peeled and chopped
½ teaspoon salt
2 green chiles, parched and peeled (page 13), chopped
1¾ cups chicken broth

1. Rinse and drain the raw rice; drain thoroughly.
2. Heat lard in a heavy skillet; add rice and brown until golden. Add the garlic and onion, and sauté until onion begins to soften.
3. Stir in remaining ingredients, bring to a boil, immediately reduce heat, and simmer over very low heat, covered, for 20 minutes.

ALMOND AND RAISIN RICE

This sweet rice is a refreshing complement to many spicy Southwestern specialties like moles and picadillo. It can be frozen for up to 3 months.

Yield: 4 servings

2¾ cups water
½ teaspoon salt
¾ cup uncooked rice
1 tablespoon natural or light brown sugar
2 tablespoons butter
½ cup raisins, coarsely chopped
½ cup slivered almonds, toasted

1. Place water, salt, rice, and sugar in a saucepan. Bring to a boil, immediately reduce heat, stir in remaining ingredients, and cover tightly.
2. Simmer very gently, without peeking, for 15 minutes, until rice is tender and fluffy.
3. Spoon into a warmed serving dish and serve immediately.

NATIVE POSOLE

A meat and vegetable combination that serves as a side dish or a very hearty main dish stew. Posole is a true native of the Southwest and is a dish that can't be hurried—start it early in the morning and let it simmer gently throughout the day to develop its true fullness of flavor. Traditionally served during the celebration of the New Year, Posole is said to bring legendary good fortune! Placed in rigid, sealed containers, posole can be frozen for up to 8 months.

Yield: 8 to 12 servings

2 cups dry posole (or 2 pounds frozen)
2 pounds pork steak or roast, cut in small cubes
1 tablespoon salt, or more to taste
2 large cloves garlic, minced
½ teaspoon ground comino (cumin)
4 tablespoons chile caribe, or substitute 4 or more
    tablespoons pure ground red chile to taste

1. Cook posole in unseasoned water until soft. Using medium-low heat, this usually requires about 2 hours. Continue adding more water as needed. Meanwhile, in a heavy pot or Dutch oven, brown the cubes of meat and then simmer in a little water until tender. Add the posole to the meat.
2. Add the remaining ingredients and allow to stew for 6 to 8 hours, *or more*. Check the water regularly, adding more as necessary.

NOTE: It is very important to note that posole *cannot* be seasoned until it becomes soft, otherwise it won't get tender. To obtain dry posole, you may have to go to a store that carries Mexican specialty foods or order by mail.

PAPAS Y CHORIZO
(POTATOES AND CHORIZO SAUSAGE)

Terrific with scrambled eggs for brunch.

Yield: 4 servings

¾ pound chorizo suasage
1 large onion, chopped
2 large potatoes, sliced in ¼-inch thick slices

1. Remove chorizo from casing, crumble, and cook in a large skillet until lightly browned. Stir in the onion and potatoes and cook over high heat to crisp the outside edges of the potatoes. Then, cover and simmer until potatoes are very tender, stirring occasionally. The potatoes will take on a wonderful reddish color from the sausage.
2. Serve piping hot.

ALBUQUERQUE HOMINY

A substitute for posole that requires less cooking. For an entree, add one pound browned chorizo when you add the Red Chile Sauce. The hominy mixture can be frozen for up to 8 months without the cheese and sausage or for 3 months with them.

Yield: 4 servings

2 tablespoons bacon drippings
1 onion, chopped
1 clove garlic, minced
1 can (18 ounces) or 2½ cups golden hominy, drained
2 large tomatoes, peeled and chopped
1 cup Red Chile Sauce (page 52)
Salt to taste
2 cups grated Monterey Jack cheese

1. Heat bacon drippings in a large skillet and sauté onion, garlic, and hominy until onion is soft.
2. Add the chopped tomatoes and simmer until almost all the liquid is gone. Stir in the Red Chile Sauce, add salt to taste, and heat thoroughly. Just before serving, stir in the cheese. Or place hominy mixture in a casserole, sprinkle cheese on top, and bake for 30 minutes at 350°F, until heated.

FRITTERS DE COLIFLOR

Batter-dipped and deep fried, fritters can be made not only with cauliflower, but with other vegetables also—green beans, carrots, corn, broccoli, green chiles, or bell peppers. Serve as a vegetable dish or as an appetizer with spicy salsa for dipping.

Yield: about 6 servings

1 head cauliflower
1 cup flour
1½ teaspoons baking powder
½ teaspoon salt
1 egg, beaten
1 cup milk, approximately
Lard or oil for deep frying
Salsa Fresca (page 50)

1. Break cauliflower into medium-size flowerettes and steam until crisp and tender. Drain thoroughly.
2. In a medium-size bowl, combine the flour, baking powder, and salt. Add the egg and milk to make a batter. Beat until smooth.
3. Heat about 3 inches of oil in a saucepan or deep fryer to 375° F. Dip the cauliflower into the batter and deep fry 3 or 4 pieces at a time until golden on all sides. Drain on paper towelling and keep warm in oven until all are fried. Serve with Salsa Fresca for dipping.

NOTE: If using corn kernels, use less milk so that the batter can be dropped by tablespoonsful into the hot fat.

GREEN BEANS AND CAULIFLOWER WITH SALSA

Serve with fish, poultry, or meat.

Yield: 6 servings

1 small head cauliflower, separated into flowerettes
1 pound fresh whole green beans, stems snipped off
Salsa Ranchero (page 58)
¾ cup shredded Monterey Jack cheese

1. Using a vegetable steamer in a saucepan, steam the vegetables until crisp and tender; do not over-cook.
2. While the vegetables are cooking, heat the Salsa Ranchero.
3. Place cooked vegetables in a warmed serving dish, pour sauce over, and sprinkle with grated cheese. Serve immediately.

CORN TORTILLAS

The classic! Tortillas can be frozen layered with wax paper and wrapped in foil or an airtight heavy plastic bag, for up to 3 months.

Yield: about 6 tortillas

1 cup masa harina (white, yellow, or blue)
½ teaspoon salt
Boiling water

1. In a mixing bowl, combine the salt and the masa and make a well in the center of these dry ingredients. Pour about ¼ cup boiling water into the well and mix, continuing to add water, a little at a time, until a very firm dough is formed. (I find it easiest to mix the dough first with a spoon and finish with my hands.) The dough should be very firm and springy, not dry and crumbly or sticky.

2. Cover the dough with a towel and let it set for about an hour.

3. Divide the dough into balls about 2 inches in diameter. To form tortillas, Mexicans use their moistened palms; most of us, however, find it easier to use a rolling pin, bolillo, or tortilla press. With a rolling pin, roll the dough between two moistened pieces of waxed paper. Be very careful not to over-moisten the waxed paper—the tortillas will stick if you do.

4. Preheat a cast-iron griddle or other heavy, dark, flat frying surface that is well seasoned. Do not add any shortening. Peel off one piece of the waxed paper from the tortilla. Place the tortilla on the hot griddle and remove the second piece of waxed paper as the tortilla begins to heat.

5. When the tortilla is hot on the top, turn on the second side for a few seconds. Stack in a warm cloth.

6. As a bread, serve warm, flat, rolled, or folded in quarters. Or fry for tostados, tacos, and other uses.

NOTE: This recipe can be doubled.

TORTILLAS DE HARINA (WHEAT TORTILLAS)

The bread staple of the border states, flour tortillas are delicious and simple to make. Once you try them you will no doubt want to keep a ready supply on hand. Wheat tortillas are the basis for burritos and chivichangos. They can be frozen, layered with wax paper and wrapped in foil or an airtight plastic bag for up to 3 months.

Yield: 4 to 6 tortillas

2 cups all-purpose flour
1 teaspoon baking powder
1 teaspoon salt
¼ teaspoon sugar (for a browner, bubbled surface)
2 tablespoons lard
¾ cup warm water

1. Combine dry ingredients; then cut in the lard with a pastry blender or your fingers.

2. Make a well in the center and add about half of the water; then add the remaining water, a few drops at a time, and work dough with your hands until a firm dough that clings together in a ball is formed. Knead the dough 15 or 20 times; then allow it to rest for 10 minutes.

3. Form the dough into egg-size balls and roll them with a rolling pin or bolillo until they are about ⅛-inch thick and 6 inches or larger in diameter.

4. For cooking tortillas, use, if possible, a hot cast-iron griddle, comal, or stove lid (known to native New Mexican cooks as a tapa). A regular griddle or frying pan can be used, but the tortillas will not brown as well. Cook each tortilla as it is rolled until it has light brown flecks on each side. Keep them warm in a cloth-lined basket until serving.

NOTE: Do not use vegetable shortening; its use will make the tortillas tough. If lard is unavailable, you can use butter.

This recipe can be doubled.

CALABACITAS PICATA (SPICY ZUCCHINI)

This recipe is also very good with yellow summer squash, chayote, and green or wax beans. It can be frozen for up to 6 months
without the addition of sour cream.

Yield: 4 servings

2 tablespoons butter
1 onion, chopped
1 clove garlic, minced
3 or 4 zucchini (each about 8 inches long), sliced
2 large tomatoes, peeled and chopped
1 teaspoon minced cilantro or parsley
2 green chiles, parched and peeled (page 13), sliced in thin
   strips
Salt
Freshly ground black pepper
1 cup grated Monterey Jack cheese
½ cup sour cream, optional

1. Melt the butter in a large skillet and sauté the onion and
garlic until onion is soft. Add the zucchini, tomatoes, cilantro,
green chiles, salt, and pepper.

2. Cover and simmer until squash is tender, about 10 to 15
minutes.

3. Place vegetables in a flameproof serving dish, sprinkle
cheese over, and place under a preheated broiler just long enough
to melt the cheese.

4. Serve immediately with dollops of sour cream spooned
over, if desired.

Pan (Breads)

Bread is an essential part of the diet in almost every culture, and the American Indians are no exception. In southwestern cooking, wheat flour is often used in bread-making, and wheat tortillas appear more often than the corn variety.

In New Mexico, sopaipillas frequently are served in place of wheat tortillas, especially in the local restaurants. These hollow puffs of golden deep-fried bread are served with lots of honey. This delicious combination has a very practical function—it very effectively dampens the fires of the hot and fiery dishes it accompanies.

In neighboring states, sopaipillas are more often served as a dessert, lavishly dusted with powdered sugar or a cinnamon and sugar mixture.

Other delicious breads include Navajo fry bread (which is similar to sopaipillas), cornbread made with blue cornmeal, Indian bear paw bread, and bolillos.

SOPAIPILLAS (DEEP-FRIED BREAD)

Sopaipillas are truly native to the Southwest, originating in Old Town, Albuquerque, over 300 years ago. These hollow puffs can be served as a bread with honey to accompany a Tex-Mex meal. They are delicious sprinkled with cinnamon and sugar as a dessert or snack and make wonderful "pocket bread" for stuffing with refried beans, chile con carne and accompaniments for a main dish sandwich.

Leftover sopaipillas can be frozen in an airtight package for up to 3 months. Reheat in a foil packet at 350°F for 15 minutes. Just before serving, open the foil to allow the sopaipillas to dry out on the outside. These puffs will be better for stuffing than for serving as a bread or dessert.

Yield: about 4 dozen small puffs

4 cups all-purpose flour
1 teaspoon baking powder
1½ teaspoons salt
1 tablespoon lard or butter
1 package active dry yeast, optional (gives pleasant yeasty aroma and a more elastic texture)
¼ cup warm water (105° F to 115°F)
1¼ cups scalded milk (approximately), cooled to room temperature
Lard or cooking oil for deep frying

1. Combine dry ingredients and cut in 1 tablespoon lard.
2. Dissolve the yeast in the warm water and add this mixture to the cooled, scalded milk. (If not using yeast, use 1½ cups milk and omit the ¼ cup water.)
3. Add about 1¼ cups liquid to dry ingredients and work into the dough. Add more liquid gradually until dough is firm and springy and holds its shape.
4. Knead dough thoroughly, for about 5 minutes, until smooth, firm, and elastic. Invert the bowl over the kneaded dough and let

rest for 10 minutes. Heat 3-inch depth of lard or oil to 400° F in a deep fryer.

5. Working with one-fourth of the dough at a time, roll to ¼-inch thickness or slightly thinner, then cut into triangles or squares; *do not* reroll any of the dough. Fry the sopaipillas, a few at a time, in the hot fat. They should puff and become hollow soon after they are immersed in the fat. Hint: To assure puffing, slightly stretch each piece of dough before frying, and place the rolled or top side of dough into the fat first, so it will become the bottom side of the sopaipilla. With tongs, hold each piece down in the fat until it puffs.

6. Drain well on paper towelling.

BLUE CORNBREAD

Blue cornmeal, used by the Pueblo Indians living along the northern Rio Grande in New Mexico, makes this cornbread special. Unfamiliar to most of us, it's very definitely blue-grey in color and owes its full, rich, nutlike flavor to piñon smoking and grinding on a lava wheel. I have always thought that blue cornmeal improves the taste of any recipe in which it is used. If you can't find blue cornmeal, it can be ordered by mail. This bread can be frozen, tightly wrapped, for up to 3 months.

Yield: one 9-inch square pan or
9 to 12 pieces

2 eggs, beaten
¾ cup milk
½ cup melted bacon drippings
1½ cups blue cornmeal
3 tablespoons sugar
1 tablespoon baking powder
½ teaspoon salt

1. Preheat oven to 350°F. Combine eggs, milk, and bacon drippings; set aside.

2. In a medium-size mixing bowl, combine the cornmeal, sugar, baking powder, and salt. Add the liquid ingredients all at once to the dry; mix only until thoroughly moistened.

3. Pour batter into a greased and floured 9-inch square pan. Bake for 30 minutes, or until bread pulls away slightly from the sides of pan and is lightly browned.

NOTE: For variety, add 3 or 4 seeded and chopped mild green chiles to the batter.

BOLILLOS (MEXICAN HARD ROLLS)

Crunchy on the outside and soft on the inside, these easy-to-make rolls should be served warm with lots of sweet butter for the best flavor. Serve with soup or stew, as dinner rolls or sandwich rolls, or for breakfast. I ate them every morning in Mexico with jam or honey. I guarantee you'll make them again and again! They can be frozen for up to 3 months.

Yield: 1 dozen rolls

¾ cup warm water (105°F to 115°F)
½ package active dry yeast (1½ teaspoons)
1 teaspoon sugar
½ teaspoon salt
3 cups all-purpose flour, approximately
Corn meal
1 egg white
1 tablespoon water

1. Pour warm water into a large, warmed mixing bowl (warm the bowl by filling with hot water and letting it set for a few minutes). Add the yeast and sugar; stir until yeast dissolves.

2. Stir in the salt, then the flour, one cup at a time, beating well after each addition. After adding the second cup, add flour gradually until dough becomes too stiff to mix with a spoon.

3. Turn out onto a floured board and knead until smooth and elastic, about 10 minutes. Place in a lightly greased bowl, grease

the top of the dough, and cover the bowl with a towel. Let rise in a warm place until doubled in bulk.

4. Punch down; let dough rise again until doubled.

5. Divide dough in half, then divide each half into six equal pieces. Shape each piece of dough into ovals about 4 inches long. Pull and twist the ends slightly. Place about 2 inches apart on a baking sheet that has been lightly sprinkled with cornmeal.

6. Make a ¼-inch deep cut lengthwise along top of each roll. Cover lightly with a towel and allow to rise again until doubled, about an hour.

7. Brush tops of rolls lightly with beaten egg white combined with water. Bake in a preheated 400°F oven for 15 minutes; remove from oven. Return to oven and bake 10 to 20 minutes longer or until lightly browned. Serve hot.

NOTE: This recipe may be doubled.

NAVAJO FRY BREAD

I have always believed that this bread inspired the seventeenth century Spaniards who settled in Albuquerque, New Mexico to create sopaipillas. The traditional hole in the center of the bread originated with the Navajo method of frying the pieces of dough on the end of a green piñon twig. To this day, fry bread is considered a very special treat at outdoor festivals, horse shows, and fairs. I can remember waiting on what seemed to be a line a quarter mile long just to get a freshly fried disk!

Fry bread is extraordinarily versatile. The Indians enjoy adding fresh herbs, like mountain oregano and crushed juniper berries, and seeds to the dough before frying. It can be served as a bread with chile dishes, or used as a basis for the popular treat, the Navajo taco, which is made by using a taco filling on top of a piece of fry bread. When freshly fried and drizzled with honey or generously dusted with raw sugar and cinnamon, fry bread becomes a delicious dessert.

Wrapped tightly, leftover fry bread can be frozen for up to three months. To reheat, follow the directions for sopaipillas (pages 196–97).

Yield: 24 pieces, approximately

4 cups all-purpose flour
3 teaspoons baking powder
1 teaspoon salt
1⅓ cups warm water, approximately
Lard or oil for deep frying
Cornmeal or flour

1. In a mixing bowl, combine flour, baking powder, and salt. Add warm water in small amounts until mixture reaches the consistency of bread dough. Knead thoroughly until smooth and elastic, cover the bowl, and let the dough rest for 10 minutes.

2. Heat 2 to 3 inches of lard or oil in a deep fryer to 400°F. Pull off 2-inch round pieces of dough and roll out ¼-inch thick and about 8 to 10 inches round on a board lightly dusted with cornmeal or flour. Punch a hole in the center of each piece.

3. Fry bread, one at a time, on each side until golden. Serve hot.

Freezing tip: Wrap airtight and freeze up to 3 months.

NOTE: The Navajo taco is another very popular Southwestern treat. To create, use any taco filling combination on top of these wonderful disks of fry bread. Enjoy!!!

INDIAN BEAR PAW BREAD

This Pueblo Indian bread that originated in the New Mexico Rio Grande area is always made in the shape of a bear's paw. It is crusty, easy to make, delicious to eat, and most impressive in appearance! In New Mexico, Indian women sell this bread as a popular souvenir in and near the pueblos, and around the plazas in Albuquerque and Santa Fe. They bake the loaves in hornos (adobe ovens). This recipe can be easily halved and can be frozen, well wrapped, for up to 3 months.

Yield: 4 loaves

2 cups hot water
2 teaspoons lard
1 teaspoon honey
½ teaspoon salt
2 packages active dry yeast (2 tablespoons)
½ cup warm water (105°F to 115°F)
10 cups all-purpose flour

1. Place 2 cups hot water, lard, honey, and salt in a large mixing bowl; stir to melt lard. Dissolve the yeast in ½ cup warm water. When mixture in bowl has cooled to room temperature, stir in yeast mixture.

2. Add the flour, one cup at a time, beating well after each addition. After 8 cups have been added to the dough, place the remaining 2 cups on a board and turn the dough out onto it. Knead until smooth and elastic, 10 to 15 minutes.

3. Place the dough in a lightly greased bowl, grease the top of the dough, cover with a towel, and let rise until doubled. Turn out on a floured board and knead again for about 3 minutes.

4. Divide dough in quarters and form each piece into a flat circle about 8 inches in diameter. Fold each circle almost in half, allowing the bottom to extend about an inch beyond the top. With a sharp knife, slash the dough twice, cutting through both layers of dough, about halfway back to the fold. This will form three

separated sections—the bear's paw. Place each loaf in a greased 9-inch pie plate, curving the folded side in a crescent shape. Separate the slashes. Cover loosely with a towel and allow to rise until doubled.

5. Preheat oven to 350°F and place a shallow pan of hot water on the bottom rack of the oven. Place loaves on the rack above so that neither is directly above the water. Bake about 1 hour, or until lightly browned.

Postres (Desserts)

Postres, served at the end of the meal, are usually quite simple in the southwestern Indian, as well as the Mexican cuisine. Most often dessert will be fresh fruit of some form or a custard or pudding, frequently accompanied by crisp, freshly baked cookies.

Cakes and pastries are typically reserved for holidays, festival treats, and other special occasions.

Refreshing ice creams and sherbets can be served with fruit empanadas, with one of the fudge sauces included in this section, or with a splash of kahlúa!

KAHLÚA CREAM PIE

Kahlúa, the liqueur of Mexico, combines with cream to make a heavenly dessert.

Yield: 6 to 8 servings

1 envelope (1 tablespoon) unflavored gelatin
½ cup cold water
½ cup sugar
⅛ teaspoon salt
3 eggs, separated
½ cup kahlúa
1½ cups heavy cream, whipped
1 baked pie crust (9-inch size)
Bizcochitos Chocolate Glaze (page 217)
Toasted sliced almonds

1. Sprinkle gelatin in cold water in a small pan. Add ¼ cup of the sugar, the salt, and the egg yolks. Stir to blend. Cook over very low heat, stirring constantly until gelatin dissolves and mixture thickens—do not boil.

2. Remove from heat and stir in the Kahlúa. Chill, stirring occasionally, until mixture is thick enough to mound on a spoon. Beat the 3 egg whites until stiff. Gradually beat the remaining ¼ cup sugar into the whites to form a glossy meringue. Fold into the gelatin mixture along with half of the whipped cream.

3. Turn into the baked pie crust. Chill thoroughly. Drizzle Bizcochitos Chocolate Glaze over top and garnish with the remaining whipped cream and the sliced almonds. Serve.

SPICED PECANS

Serve with coffee and dessert or sprinkle over ice cream and Mexican Fudge Sauce (pages 214–15) for a super sundae!

Yield: 2¹/₂ cups

2 tablespoons cold water
1 egg white
¹/₂ cup sugar
¹/₂ teaspoon salt
¹/₄ teaspoon ground cloves
¹/₂ teaspoon ground cinnamon
¹/₄ teaspoon ground allspice
2¹/₂ cups whole pecan halves

1. Add water to egg white and beat until foamy. Add sugar and spices and stir well. Let stand until sugar dissolves, about 15 minutes; then stir until well mixed. Preheat oven to 300°F.

2. Add nuts and stir until well mixed; place on large flat baking pan.

3. Bake in oven, stirring after 20 minutes. Then bake for 15 minutes longer and stir well. Bake for another 5 or 10 minutes, watching carefully to make certain the nuts just glaze—they should not be sugary or over-browned. Recipe usually takes about 45 minutes to bake.

VARIATION: Substitute almonds, walnuts, or peanuts, if desired.

INDIAN BREAD PUDDING

Rich and satisfying. This pudding can be frozen, tightly wrapped, for up to 2 months.

Yield: 6 to 8 servings

Half of a 1-pound loaf of firm, white bread, sliced
4 tablespoons butter, softened
1½ cups dark brown sugar
3 cups water
2 whole cloves
1 piece cinnamon stick (3 inches long), or 1 teaspoon ground cinnamon
2 eggs
½ cup slivered almonds
½ cup walnuts, chopped
1 teaspoon vanilla
1 apple, peeled and sliced in thin wedges
1 cup raisins
½ cup milk or light cream
1 cup grated Monterey Jack cheese

1. Butter the bread slices, place on a baking sheet, and bake 15 minutes at 350°F, until toasted. Set aside to cool; then cut in cubes.
2. Boil brown sugar, water, cloves, and cinnamon stick in a saucepan until slightly thickened, about 5 minutes. Remove from heat, take out the cloves and cinnamon stick, and set aside.
3. In a bowl, beat together the eggs, almonds, walnuts, vanilla, apple slices, raisins, and milk or light cream.
4. Place half the bread cubes in a buttered baking dish or casserole. Spoon half the egg/fruit/nut mixture on top; then half the grated cheese. Repeat, ending with a layer of grated cheese.
5. Pour the syrup over and bake at 350°F for 30 to 45 minutes, until the liquid is absorbed and the pudding is firm.
6. Serve warm, topped with whipped cream or ice cream.

PLATANOS BAKED IN ORANGE SYRUP

Yield: 4 to 8 servings

¼ cup butter
4 large plantains (cooking bananas), peeled and sliced in half
    lengthwise
3 tablespoons flour
1 cup brown sugar
2 tablespoons rum
Juice of 1½ oranges
½ orange, thinly sliced
¾ cup powdered sugar
¾ cup sour cream

1. Heat butter in a large, heavy skillet and brown the bananas slightly on each side. Place bananas and remaining butter from pan in a baking dish.

2. Mix 3 tablespoons flour with the brown sugar and sprinkle over the bananas. Add the rum and orange juice; arrange orange slices over top.

3. Bake in a preheated 375°F oven for about 20 minutes, or until plantains are tender. Meanwhile, combine the powdered sugar and sour cream.

4. Serve baked plantains warm with sweetened sour cream sauce spooned over.

FROZEN LIME CREAM

Wonderfully easy to prepare and deliciously refreshing and soothing.

Yield: 1 pint

1 cup whole milk
1 cup heavy cream
1 cup sugar
Juice and rind of 1 lime
Green food coloring, if desired

1. Combine milk, cream, and sugar in a mixing bowl. Stir and place in freezer. Stirring periodically, freeze until mixture becomes slushy and sugar is dissolved.
2. Fold in the lime juice and rind and a drop of green food coloring. Poor sherbet in a container and freeze until firm.

VARIATIONS: Use juice and rind of 2 lemons, or the rind of 1 orange and a little frozen orange juice concentrate.

FLAN (CARAMEL CUSTARD)

Of Spanish origin and a favorite throughout Mexico. A most traditional dessert.

Yield: 6 servings

2 tablespoons water
1¼ cups sugar (½ cup for caramel, ¾ cup for flan)
6 eggs
3¼ cups milk
¼ teaspoon cinnamon (optional)
1 teaspoon vanilla

1. Preheat oven to 350°F.

2. Place 2 tablespoons water and ½ cup of the sugar in a heavy skillet. Heat over medium heat until sugar is melted and caramelized. Immediately pour caramelized sugar into a 6-cup round baking dish (or six custard cups) and tilt the dish so caramel comes slightly up the side of the dish. Caramel will harden but softens as flan is baking.

3. Beat together thoroughly the remaining ¾ cup sugar and the eggs. Beat in the milk, cinnamon, and vanilla. (Or place eggs, sugar, milk, and flavorings in blender container and blend for 1 minute.)

4. Pour custard into caramel-lined dish or custard cups. Set in a pan filled with ½ inch of hot water and bake for 1 hour and 15 minutes, or until knife inserted in the center comes out clean.

5. Chill *thoroughly* for at least 3 hours. To unmold, run a knife around the side of the flan, place a serving dish over the mold, and invert quickly.

VARIATIONS:

Flan de Café: Add 1 rounded teaspoon instant coffee dissolved in 1 tablespoon boiling water to the custard mixture.

Almond Flan: Add ½ teaspoon almond extract and ½ cup blanched ground almonds.

Pecan Flan: Sprinkle 1 cup coarsely chopped pecans on top of the caramelized sugar in the mold before pouring in the custard.

FLAN DE COCO (COCONUT FLAN)

Sweet and delicious. I use an 8-inch cast-iron skillet to caramelize the sugar and bake the flan right in the same skillet.

Yield: 4 to 6 servings

¼ cup sugar
2 tablespoons water
½ cup grated coconut
1 can (13½ ounces) evaporated milk
3 eggs
¾ cup sugar
1 teaspoon coconut extract

1. Place ¼ cup sugar and 1 tablespoon water in a heavy skillet and place on medium-high heat. Mix until the sugar melts and browns, then quickly pour into an 8-inch pie plate, tilting the pie plate so that caramel goes slightly up the sides of the pan. Caramel will harden.

2. Sprinkle caramel with the grated coconut.

3. Combine remaining ingredients in a bowl, beat well, and pour over the coconut. Cover the pie plate with foil and place in a pan with ½ inch of boiling water in it.

4. Bake in a preheated 350°F oven for 1 hour. Remove the foil for last ½ hour of baking.

5. Cool; chill *thoroughly* for at least 3 hours. Unmold by running a knife around the sides of the custard; place a serving plate over the mold and invert quickly. The flan should just plop right out of the pan.

APRICOT EMPANADAS

These empanadas are baked rather than deep fried. Make them large or small and use other dried fruits for variety. Serve warm with ice cream, pack for picnics and lunch box desserts, or have ready for mid-afternoon snacks or tea. They can be frozen, baked or unbaked, for up to 6 months.

Yield: about 3 dozen large or
4¹/₂ dozen small turnovers

Apricot Filling

½ pound dried apricots (or dried peaches, nectarines, apples, or pears)
2 cups water
¾ to 1¼ cups sugar
½ cup raisins soaked in 1 cup hot water, drained
1 teaspoon cinnamon
½ teaspoon nutmeg
¼ teaspoon salt

1. Place dried apricots, water, and sugar in a saucepan. Bring to a boil, cover, and simmer gently until very soft, about 45 minutes, adding a little more water, if necessary. Drain fruit, reserving the syrup, and cool.

2. Chop the cooked apricots and combine with remaining ingredients, adding reserved apricot syrup, if needed, to make a moist filling.

Pastry

2 cups flour
1 teaspoon baking powder
½ teaspoon salt
⅛ teaspoon ground coriander seed (optional)
½ cup shortening, lard, or butter
⅓ cup milk or water

1. Combine flour, baking powder, salt, and coriander seed in a bowl. Cut in shortening until mixture is crumbly. Add milk or water gradually until dough holds together and forms a ball.

2. Preheat oven to 450°F. Roll pastry on a floured board to thickness of about ⅛ inch. Cut in rounds. Place a little filling in center of each, moisten edges of pastry, and fold over. Crimp the edges to seal or press with the tines of a fork.

3. Place empanadas on a baking sheet and bake until golden, about 10 minutes. Serve warm or at room temperature.

RIO GRANDE EMPANADAS

These mincemeat dessert turnovers are made with an unrisen yeast dough crust and are deep fried. They are typical festival and holiday fare in southern New Mexico. Bet you can't eat just one! Freeze before or after frying for up to 4 months. Reheat previously fried empanadas by placing on a baking sheet in a 400°F oven for 10 minutes.

*Yield: about 6 dozen small or
4 dozen large
empanadas*

Mincemeat Filling

1½ pounds beef for boiling (an inexpensive cut)
½ cup molasses
¾ cup sugar
1 teaspoon salt
¾ teaspoon crushed coriander seed
1 tablespoon ground cloves
1 teaspoon cinnamon
1 cup applesauce
1¼ cups raisins
3½ cups chopped nuts (walnuts, piñons, or almonds)
⅓ cup dry sherry or brandy

1. Place meat in a pan; add water to cover. Bring to a boil,

cover pan, and simmer until tender. Drain. Grind with a meat grinder or in a blender or food processor.

2. Combine meat with remaining ingredients and let rest for several hours or overnight to blend flavors. The mixture should be moist and thick—if it seems dry, add a little more liquid.

Pastry

3¾ cups flour
¾ teaspoon salt
2 teaspoons sugar
¼ cup lard (or shortening)
1 teaspoon dry yeast
½ cup warm water (105°F to 115°F), approximately

1. Combine flour, salt, and sugar; cut in lard.
2. Dissolve the dry yeast in the ½ cup warm water and mix into the dry ingredients to make a stiff dough. A little more water may be needed. Do not let the dough rise.
3. On a floured board, roll the dough to a thickness of ⅛ inch, and cut into 3-inch rounds (or larger, depending on size of empanadas desired).
4. To assemble the empanadas, place a small amount of filling in center of each round, moisten the edge of pastry, fold over and press to seal. Crimp the edges or press with the tines of a fork to make a tight seal.
5. Deep fry the pies in oil preheated to 400°F (use a thermometer or an electric deep fryer), until golden, about 2 minutes on each side. Fry only a few at a time so that the 400°F temperature is maintained.
6. Drain on paper toweling. Dust with powdered sugar and serve warm with whipped cream or ice cream.

MEXICAN FUDGE SAUCE I

Sold in most Mexican specialty shops, Mexican chocolate has a unique flavor and consistency. It is already sweetened, has a granular texture, and is spiced with cinnamon, nutmeg, and cloves.

Make parfaits by layering kahlúa, ice cream, and Fudge Sauce in a goblet, or drizzle Fudge Sauce over fresh strawberries or other fruits and top with a dollop of whipped or sour cream. A special added touch is a sprinkling of Spiced Pecans (page 205).

Keep a good-sized batch on hand in the refrigerator—it will keep for up to two months.

Yield: 1¹/₄ cups

4 squares (4 ounces) Mexican chocolate
1 cup light or medium cream

1. Place the Mexican chocolate in a small, heavy saucepan set over low heat and stir until it is melted.
2. Add the cream very slowly, stirring constantly to mix evenly. Heat but do not boil.
3. Serve the sauce warm over ice cream or drizzle over Mexican Pecan Cake (page 217).

MEXICAN FUDGE SAUCE II

If Mexican chocolate is unavailable to you, try this fudge sauce.
Store leftover sauce in a covered container in the refrigerator. If sauce becomes too thick with holding, thin slightly by adding a little boiling water.

Yield: 3 cups

1 can (14½ ounces) evaporated milk
1¾ cups sugar
4 ounces (4 squares) unsweetened chocolate
¼ cup butter
1 teaspoon vanilla
½ teaspoon salt
1 teaspoon cinnamon
¼ teaspoon cloves
⅛ teaspoon nutmeg

1. Heat milk and sugar, stirring constantly, until mixture simmers.
2. Add the chocolate and stir until melted. Beat until smooth (if sauce has slightly curdled appearance, beat vigorously—it will become creamy smooth).
3. Remove from heat and stir in the butter, vanilla, salt, cinnamon, cloves, and nutmeg. Serve warm.

BIZCOCHITOS

These spicy, anise-flavored cookies from New Mexico are rich, crisp, and very easy to make. And they make wonderful ice cream sandwiches—a cookie on the bottom, vanilla ice cream in the middle, and another cookie on top! These cookies are my holiday favorite.

Stored in a tightly sealed container, these cookies will freeze for up to 6 months.

Yield: about 4 dozen

1½ cups butter or lard
1 cup sugar
2 eggs
2 teaspoons anise seed
4 cups flour
2 teaspoons baking powder
½ teaspoon salt
3 tablespoons brandy, approximately (or use apple juice or milk)
3 tablespoons sugar
2 teaspoons cinnamon

1. Cream together the butter or lard and sugar until fluffy. Add the eggs and anise seed and beat again until very light and fluffy.

2. Sift together the flour, baking powder, and salt. Add to creamed mixture along with the brandy. Mix thoroughly to make a stiff dough.

3. Roll dough on a floured board to ¼-inch thickness, and cut with cutters into cookie designs or into 3-inch rounds.

4. Combine the 3 tablespoons sugar and 2 teaspoons cinnamon and sprinkle over tops of unbaked cookies. Place on cookie sheets and bake in a preheated 350°F oven until lightly browned, about 10 to 12 minutes.

5. Cool cookies on wire racks and "frost" with Bizcochitos Chocolate Glaze (recipe follows).

BIZCOCHITOS CHOCOLATE GLAZE: In a small saucepan, combine 6 ounces semisweet chocolate morsels, 1½ tablespoons vegetable shortening, and 1 teaspoon vanilla. Heat gently until melted and smooth, stirring constantly. Cool slightly and dip a corner of each cookie into the glaze.

MEXICAN PECAN CAKE

This rich pound cake is excellent topped with Butter-Lemon Glaze or with Mexican Fudge Sauce (pages 214–15). It will freeze well for up to 6 months.

Yield: 10 to 12 servings

1½ cups sugar
⅔ cup ground pecans (or almonds)
¼ teaspoon salt
1 cup butter (½ pound)
1 tablespoon lemon juice
5 eggs
1¾ cups sifted flour

1. Place sugar, pecans, salt, butter, and lemon juice in a mixing bowl. With an electric mixer, cream mixture very well, until fluffy.
2. Add the eggs and beat thoroughly until mixture is very light and airy. Add the flour and beat well again.
3. Spoon batter into a greased and floured 10-inch spring-form pan and bake in a preheated 325°F oven for about 1 hour, or until cake tests done.
4. Cool and serve with warm Butter-Lemon Glaze drizzled over.

Butter-Lemon Glaze

¼ cup butter
1 cup honey or sugar
5 teaspoons lemon juice
¼ cup coarsely chopped pecans

1. Combine butter, honey, and lemon juice in a small pan. Boil gently for 2 minutes, remove from heat, cool for 10 minutes, stir in the pecans, and drizzle over cooled cake.

TAMALES DE DULCE I—SWEET DESSERT TAMALES

Rarely seen north of the border, these tamales are super for the holidays!

They can be frozen before steaming for up to 1 year. Remove from freezer, thaw, and steam just prior to serving.

Yield: 12 to 16 tamales
(4 to 6 servings)

2½ cups prepared Tamale Masa (pages 138–39)
½ cup sugar
1 teaspoon cinnamon
½ cup ground almonds
¾ cup raisins
12 to 16 corn husks, soaked in hot water to soften

1. Combine the prepared masa, sugar, cinnamon, and ground almonds.
2. Spread about 3 tablespoons sweet masa mixture in a line down the center of each soaked corn husk. Top mixture with a sprinkling of raisins.
3. Fold and tie corn husks (see instructions on page 137). Steam over water, not in, for 45 to 50 minutes.

VARIATION: Omit the raisins, and spread masa mixture with 2 teaspoons of raspberry or strawberry preserves. Roll, tie, and steam.

TAMALES DE DULCE II—SWEET DESSERT TAMALES

Pink and pretty, sweet and flavorful.

They can be frozen before steaming for up to 1 year. Remove from freezer, thaw, and steam just prior to serving.

Yield: 12 to 16 tamales
(4 to 6 servings)

2⅓ cups prepared Tamale Masa (pages 138–39)
1 tablespoon grenadine syrup
½ cup sugar
¾ cup golden raisins
¼ cup candied citron, finely chopped
¼ cup blanched, slivered almonds
12 to 16 corn husks, soaked in hot water to soften

1. Sweeten the prepared tamale masa with 1 tablespoon grenadine and ½ cup sugar. Add the raisins, citron, and almonds; mix.

2. Spread about 3 tablespoons masa mixture in a line down the center of each softened corn husk.

3. Fold and tie corn husks (see instructions on page 137). Steam over water, not in, for 45 to 50 minutes.

BUÑUELOS—FRITTERS IN SYRUP

When making Sopaipillas (pages 196–97), roll some of the dough into rounds and make Buñuelos. Traditionally a Christmas treat in Mexico, Buñuelos are very special and well worth the time it takes to prepare them.

Yield: about 2 dozen

²/₃ cup brown sugar
½ cup sherry
½ cup water
½ cup raisins
⅛ teaspoon anise seeds (optional)
1 teaspoon cinnamon
½ recipe for Sopaipillas (pages 196–97)

1. In a small saucepan, combine the sugar, sherry, water, raisins, anise seeds, and cinnamon. Bring to a boil and cook until slightly thickened.

2. Break off walnut-size pieces of dough and roll them into rounds on a floured board (¼-inch thick or slightly thinner). Deep fry and drain according to directions for Sopaipillas.

3. Dip the warm Buñuelos in the warm sauce and place them in a bowl. Serve warm with extra syrup for spooning over.

MEXICO CITY BUÑUELOS

These crisp, deep-fried cookies are very much like Swedish rosettes. Light and airy and very simple to make if you have the necessary cookie iron or rosette iron, the batter is done in about 45 seconds! Layered between sheets of waxed paper in a tightly sealed rigid container, Buñuelos will freeze for up to 6 months.

Yield: 3 to 6 dozen cookies,
depending on size

Vegetable oil for frying
2 cups water
1 egg
2½ cups flour
½ cup sugar
2½ tablespoons cinnamon

1. Place oil for deep frying in a large saucepan or electric deep-fat fryer. Place the rosette iron in the oil and heat to 375°F.
2. Place water, egg, and flour in a mixing bowl or blender container, and beat or blend until very smooth.
3. Remove the hot iron from the oil and quickly dip it into the batter, being careful to allow batter to reach *only* to the top of the iron (do not dip iron deep into the batter or the cookie won't release from the iron when it's frying). Immediately lower the iron into the hot oil until the cookie slips off the iron. Fry only a few at a time for about 2 minutes each, until lightly golden.
4. Drain on paper towels and sprinkle with a sugar and cinnamon mixture or with powdered sugar.

SOUTHWESTERN
HOSPITALITY

Seasonal Fiesta/Buffet Menus

Southwestern food is perfect party food. Colorful, exotic, spicy, it lends a festive touch that makes any occasion a memorable affair, be it a party, picnic, or informal family dinner.

Set the mood with some colorful touches from the "Sun Country": a paper piñata, paper flowers, pottery dishes, a woven table cloth, baskets, and a centerpiece of tropical fruits and vegetables.

I've created menus in tune with the seasons, from an outdoor summer buffet to a winter holiday cocktail party. If you follow the schedule for advance preparation after each menu, you'll be able to enjoy the party along with your guests. It's always a good idea to keep your freezer stocked with basic ingredients like green chiles, beans, posole, tortillas, salsas, and grated cheese. With these items on hand, you can whip up a fiesta meal for the family or for that unexpected guest whenever the mood strikes you.

Let this section be your guide to creating new menus and taste experiences. Salud!

(SUMMER)

FIESTA! OUTDOOR SUMMER BUFFET

Texas Punch (p. 46)

———

Roasted Cashews and Almonds
Tostadas (p. 99) and Dips:
Salsa Fresca (p. 50)
Guacamole (p. 26)
Mushrooms and Onions en Escabeche (p. 79)

———

Taco Bar With All the Fixin's (pp. 96–97)
Frijoles (p. 182)

———

Kahlúa Cream Pie (p. 204)

Two days before: Prepare meat fillings for tacos and fry the taco shells, storing them in an airtight container. Make the marinated mushrooms and tostadas. Cook the beans.

The day before: Organize the condiments for the taco bar: slice and chop vegetables, prepare salsas, and grate cheese. Make the pie and keep it chilled. Organize the taco bar table by planning which baskets, bowls, and platters will be used.

The day of the buffet: A couple of hours before, make the punch (don't add the carbonated beverage or ice until your first guest arrives). For the best flavor, make the Guacamole just before serving. Heat taco shells, fillings and beans.

(SUMMER)

PICNIC

Chilled Mexican Beer
Beef Jerky (p. 30)

———

Gazpacho (p. 68)
Bean Stuffed Avocados (p. 74)
Navajo Fry Bread (pp. 199–200)

———

Fresh Tropical Fruits/Fresh Squeezed Lime Juice
Rio Grande Empanadas (pp. 213–14)

Two days ahead: Prepare the beef jerky and the empanadas (but don't fry the empanadas until the day of the picnic).

The day before: Prepare the bean stuffing for the avocados and make the gazpacho. Prepare the fruits for dessert and pack in a sealed container.

The day of the picnic: Fry the empanadas. Shortly before leaving, make the fry bread, drain it, wrap it in foil and then in several layers of newspaper to keep it warm. Halve the avocados and fill with stuffing while at the picnic.

(SUMMER)

THE BIG BARBECUE

Frozen Daiquiris (p. 40)
Nachos Grande (p. 24)

———

Carne Asada Kabobs (p. 94)
Posole (p. 187)
Your Favorite Green Salad
Indian Bear Paw Bread (pp. 201–02)
Sweet Butter

———

Coconut Flan (p. 210)
Fruit
Coffee

Two days before: Make the hominy, reserving the cheese for stirring into the dish just before serving.

The day before: Make the flan, marinate the meat chunks, and prepare vegetables for kabobs. Grate cheese for nachos.

The day of the barbecue: Bake the bread. A few hours before serving, tear greens and slice other ingredients for the salad, assemble the kabobs, and assemble Nachos Grande platter. Just before guests arrive, place daiquiri ingredients in blender.

(FALL)

BRUNCH

Tequila Sunrise (p. 38)
Bloody Maria (p. 39)

———

Huevos Rancheros (p. 144)
Wheat Flour Tortillas (p. 195) or Bolillos (pp. 198–99)
Sweet Butter and Assorted Jams

———

Mexican Coffee (p. 48)

The day before: Make the tortillas, bolillos, and the sauce for the Huevos Rancheros. Grate the cheese and slice the scallions.

During the party: While drinks are being served, warm the sauce, the breads, and the plates. Make the coffee. At serving time, simply fry or poach the eggs, assemble the Huevos Rancheros, and garnish the plates.

(FALL)

LATE SUPPER
(AFTER FOOTBALL GAME,
TENNIS, ETC.)

Chile Quesadillas (p. 32)
Carnitas (p. 29)

————

Enchiladas Suisas (p. 120)
Hot Corn Tortillas (p. 194)
Green Salad

————

Flan (pp. 208–09)
Spiced Pecans (p. 205)

A day or two ahead: Make the wheat tortillas for the quesadillas. Prepare the salsa, shredded meat, and grated cheese for the enchiladas. Make the Carnitas, Flan, and Spiced Pecans.

The morning of the party: Make the Quesadillas; fry them if you like, and reheat them just before serving. Assemble the salad except for the dressing. Prepare the enchiladas to the point of pouring the cream on top; refrigerate until ready to use.

At serving time: Pour the cream over the enchiladas and bake. Heat foil-wrapped tortillas at the same time.

(FALL)

FRUIT OF THE SEA DINNER BUFFET

Cocktails

Guacamole and Cauliflower Salad (p. 77)*
Tostadas (p. 99)

Southwestern Zucchini Soup (p. 65)
Shrimp in Nut Sauce (pp. 168–69)
Steamed Green Beans
Rice
Bolillos (pp. 198–99) and Sweet Butter

Platanos Baked in Orange Syrup (p. 207)
Coffee

The day before: Make the soup, marinate the cauliflower for the hors d'oeuvre, and prepare the green beans. Fry the tostadas.

The morning of the buffet: Prepare nut sauce; refrigerate until baking time. Prepare dessert to the point of baking. Prepare bolillos dough.

A couple of hours before: Begin rice preparation to the point of browning. All you have to do then at dinner time is add the broth and tomato and simmer until fluffy and tender.

Just before the guests arrive: Prepare the guacamole for the cauliflower hors d'oeuvre. Preheat oven for baking bolillos just before serving.

---

* Serve this as an hors d'oeuvre with the marinated cauliflower for dipping rather than the guacamole sauce poured over.

231

(WINTER)

HOLIDAY COCKTAIL PARTY

Almost everything on this menu can be prepared in advance—at least to the point of baking, broiling, or reheating. The only exception is the Guacamole which should be done just prior to the arrival of your guests.

Cocktails

———

Taquitos con Guacamole (p. 28)
Chile Quesadillas (p. 32)
Mushrooms and Onions en Escabeche (p. 79)
Tostadas (p. 99)
Assorted Salsas (pp. 49–61)
Seafood Campeche-Style (p. 103)
Chorizo Quiche (pp.149–50)
*Carne Adobada (p. 163), thinly sliced and served with hot Wheat and
Corn Tortillas (p. 194)*

———

Fresh Fruit Assortment or Compote
Bizcochitos with Chocolate Glaze (pp. 216–17)
Mexico City Buñuelos (p. 221)

Three or more days ahead: Prepare taquitos. They freeze very well, either cooked or uncooked, so you can make them well ahead. Prepare assorted salsas. Make Carne Adobada, marinate overnight, and cook the next day. Fry the tortillas for tostada chips, seal in airtight container, and re-warm just prior to serving. Make cookies—Bizcochitos and Mexico City Buñuelos.

Two days ahead: Make the Mushrooms and Onions en Escabeche. Make corn and wheat tortillas.

The day before: Make shell for Chorizo Quiche—cover and store until baking time. Prepare the egg custard for the quiche and refrigerate until time to pour into the shell and bake. Assemble the Chile Quesadillas.

The morning of the party: Marinate Seafood Campeche-Style. Assemble fruit compote. Organize table setting and all serving pieces.

Just before guests arrive: Prepare guacamole. Wrap wheat and corn tortillas in foil and warm in the oven.

(SPRING)

A DINNER TO CELEBRATE THE END OF WINTER

Cocktails

Ceviche (p. 27)
Salsa Fresca (p. 50)
Tostadas (p. 99)

Pork Loin en Salsa Verde (pp. 164–65)
Chiles Rellenos de Queso (p. 126)
Mexican Fried Rice (p. 184)
Mixed Green Salad with Oil and Vinegar Dressing
Bolillos (pp. 198–99) and Sweet Butter

Frozen Lime Cream (p. 208)
Mexico City Buñuelos (p. 221)

A few days ahead: Make frozen lime cream and buñuelos. Fry tostadas, wrap airtight, and re-warm before serving.

The day before: Make Ceviche (marinating overnight is excellent). Prepare salsa fresca. Assemble chiles rellenos, but don't make the batter until day of dinner.

The day of the dinner: Prepare bolillo dough for baking just before serving time. Rice can be fried earlier in the day. Prepare and refrigerate salad greens. Make the salsa verde for the roast. Batter dip and fry chiles rellenos at serving time.

(SPRING)

KIDS' DINNER BUFFET

Beverage

———————

Chile con Queso (p. 31)
Tostadas (p. 99)

———————

Southwest "Pizzas" (p. 25)

———————

Bizcochitos Ice Cream Sandwiches (p. 216)

A few days ahead: Bake Bizcochitos and assemble ice cream sandwiches; wrap and freeze. Fry tostadas.

The day before: Make Chile con Queso. Prepare toppings for "pizzas" and place in bowls.

At serving time: Warm Chile con Queso and Tostadas. Place "pizzas" briefly under broiler before serving.

(SPRING)

LUNCHEON

Blonde Sangria (p. 45)

Crabmeat, Shrimp, and Avocado Salad (p. 78)
Sliced Tomatoes and Cucumbers
Hot Wheat Tortillas or Bolillos (pp. 195, 198–99)

Mexican Pecan Cake with Ice Cream (p. 217)
Coffee   Tea

The day before: Bake the cake and make the tortillas.

The day of the Luncheon: Prepare bolillo dough for baking just before serving. Prepare the sangria shortly before guests arrive. Wrap tortillas in foil for warming and slice the tomatoes and cucumbers. Assemble ingredients for the seafood. Luncheon entree takes only a very few minutes to prepare.

Mail-Order Sources

Some of the ingredients called for in the recipes may be difficult to find at your local supermarket, such as pure chile powder, blue cornmeal, posole, and masa. When I encountered this problem, I solved it by starting the Pecos Valley Spice Company for Mexican Cooking. Since I don't expect you to do the same, the following is a list of mail order sources that you will find helpful.

ADOBE HOUSE
127 Payne Street
  Dallas, Tex. 75207
  (214) 748-0983

ASHLEY'S MEXICAN FOODS
  Division, Bruce Foods Corp.
  P.O. Drawer 1030
  New Iberia, La. 70560
  (318) 365-8101

CASADOS FARMS/DOS VES, INC.
  Box 1269
  San Juan Pueblo, N. Mex. 87566

CASA MONEO
  210 W. 14th Street
  New York, N.Y. 10011

EL MOLINO TAMALES
  117 S. 22nd Street
  Phoenix, Ariz. 85034
  (602) 244-0364

H. ROTH AND SON
  1577 First Avenue
  New York, N.Y. 10021

JANE BUTEL'S PECOS VALLEY SPICE CO.
  142 Lincoln Avenue
  Santa Fe, N. Mex. 87051
  800-Hot Taco

LA SEMILLERA HORTICULTURAL ENTERPRISES
  P.O. Box 34082
  Dallas, Tex. 75234

SASABE STORE
  "Hot Stuff"
  P.O. Box 7
  Sasabe, Ariz. 85704

SIMON DAVID GROCERY STORE
  7117 Inwood Road
  Dallas, Tex. 78207
  (214) 352-1781

TAOS CHILI COMPANY
  Turley Mill Building
  Box 1100 B.A.
  Taos, N. Mex. 87571

TIA MIA
  Dept. BA 03
  Sunland Park, N. Mex. 88063

INDEX

Index

THE
COOKERY
COLLECTION
From Pocket Books

____ **THE GOURMET GUIDE TO BEER** 46197/$5.95
Howard Hillman

____ **COMPLETE VEGETARIAN COOKBOOK** 44139/$2.75
Karen Brooks

____ **CROCKERY COOKERY** 47671/$3.50
Paula Franklin

____ **DIET SIMPLY . . . WITH SOUP** 46428/$4.95
Gail Becker, R.D.

____ **DR. MANDELL'S ALLERGY-FREE COOKBOOK**
49562/$3.50 Fran Gare Mandell

____ **FEARLESS COOKING AGAINST THE CLOCK**
47641/$3.95 Michele Evans

____ **FEARLESS COOKING FOR ONE** 49294/$4.95
Michele Evans

____ **FOOD PROCESSOR COOKBOOK** 42284/$2.95
Editors of Consumer Guide

____ **KEEP IT SIMPLE** 44397/$3.95
Marian Burros

____ **THE WAY OF HERBS** 46686/$4.95
Michael Tierra

____ **WOMAN'S DAY BOOK OF BAKING** 46945/$2.95

____ **WOMAN'S DAY COLLECTOR'S COOKBOOK**
46946/$2.95

____ **WOMAN'S DAY BOOK OF NEW
MEXICAN COOKING (trade size)** 44672/$5.95

POCKET BOOKS, Department CCC
1230 Avenue of the Americas, New York, N.Y. 10020

Please send me the books I have checked above. I am enclosing
$_____ (please add 75¢ to cover postage and handling for each order.
N.Y.S. and N.Y.C. residents please add appropriate sales tax). Send check
or money order—no cash or C.O.D.'s please. Allow up to six weeks for
delivery. For purchases over $10.00, you may use VISA: card number,
expiration date and customer signature must be included.

NAME _____

ADDRESS _____

CITY _____ STATE/ZIP _____
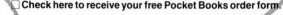
848
☐ **Check here to receive your free Pocket Books order form.**

Home delivery from Pocket Books

Here's your opportunity to have fabulous bestsellers delivered right to you. Our free catalog is filled to the brim with the newest titles plus the finest in mysteries, science fiction, westerns, cookbooks, romances, biographies, health, psychology, humor—every subject under the sun. Order this today and a world of pleasure will arrive at your door.

POCKET BOOKS, Department ORD
1230 Avenue of the Americas, New York, N.Y. 10020

Please send me a free Pocket Books catalog for home delivery

NAME _____

ADDRESS _____

CITY _____ STATE/ZIP _____

If you have friends who would like to order books at home, we'll send them a catalog too—

NAME _____

ADDRESS _____

CITY _____ STATE/ZIP _____

NAME _____

ADDRESS _____

CITY _____ STATE/ZIP _____